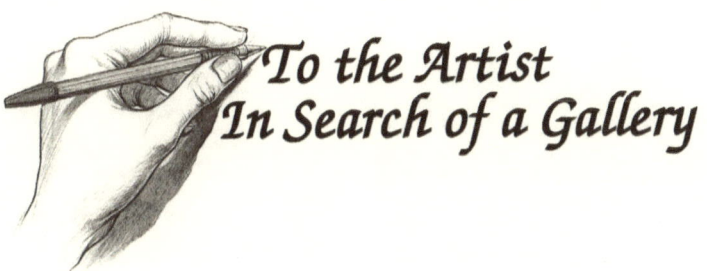

To the Artist
In Search of a Gallery

To the Artist
In Search of a Gallery
by RL Foster

Innovative Books
Denver, Colorado

Innovative Books
2014

To the Artist
In Search of a Gallery
By RL Foster

Innovative Books
P.O. Box 221734
Denver, Colorado 80222

info@innovativebooks.net

ISBN
9780692254738

Contents

Appendixes

Introduction

I joined my first art gallery over twenty years ago. The gallery was one of the most prestigious in Denver, and many artists, both local and national, sought to be represented by us. The gallery maintained an established policy for artists who wished to be considered by the gallery for representation. The policy was fairly standard for galleries at the time and I would call it the "traditional policy." Artist consultants and counselors offered workshops that presented this traditional approach to artists.

Although we contended this was the official way to be considered for the gallery, I am hard pressed to remember a single artist who was ever recruited into the gallery using the official process. Every year, we would add a half-dozen artists to our roster, but they were artists whom we recruited — not those who recruited us. I wondered if that experience was unique to our gallery or was it prevalent in the gallery community. To find the answer to this, I would query artists when I learned they had just joined a new gallery. I would ask them how that occurred. I was not really surprised to learn that they rarely succeeded by using the traditional approach, and, in fact, many of the artists succeeded by actually violating some of the precepts of the traditional method.

A decade later when I opened my own gallery, I was tempted to apply the same hypocritical, new artist policy to my gallery. Instead, I instituted a policy of allowing artists to present themselves every Wednesday. I soon realized that the situation was becoming out of hand when a dozen new artists would show up every Wednesday.

This personal experience has also clarified some thoughts on the reality facing galleries in regard to new artists.

Galleries are always seeking new artists, but there's not enough time to interview all of the artists who would like to be interviewed.

Taking my own gallery experience and the experiences of dozens of artists, I developed a workshop *To the Artist in Search of a Gallery*. I wanted to provide artists insights on how galleries actually recruited artists, and not how they claimed to recruit them. The workshops were invaluable to me in that I had an opportunity to hear artists recount their own painful experiences.

Many of the tactics and strategies that were being recommended by artist consultants were not only ineffectual, but often were counterproductive. In many cases, the wrong ways turned out to be the right ways. Because all galleries and managers do not operate in the same manner, there is no sure-fire way to successfully approach every gallery. Nor are all artists the same. Two artists may paint identically, but their personalities may be totally different. The recruiting tactics that will work for the extrovert may be impossible for the introvert.

The dominant theme in my workshop is that if the artist can get their work before gallery decision-makers, then he or she has done the job. The traditional approach does not do a good job in achieving this end. Artists have to be more creative in their thinking and execution of their plans. The workshop outlined different campaigns to reach the managers in their targeted galleries. The tactics and the strategies also could be modified for the personality of the artist.

It has been ten years since I began these workshops, and in that time, the basic principles outlined in my workshop still remain intact. If anything, the appearance of the internet has reduced the effectiveness of the established approach even more. The traditional method only works with traditional managers, and they are becoming a dying breed as digital technology is rapidly changing how galleries do business. This same digital technology has provided artists with new and better tools to do everything better, including recruiting galleries. Thus, I have had to adapt the workshop to recognize the digital reality.

In the process of restructuring my workshop, I made the decision to write this book to reflect these new realities. Again, the basic premises are still valid, but the tools have greatly expanded.

Not every artist who reads this book is going to succeed in recruiting galleries to represent him or her. The reason is obvious — not all artists paint compelling and saleable pieces. What this book will do is provide the artist with strategies and tactics to help s/he get work before gallery directors. After that, the art has to do the selling.

How to read this book

The chapters in this book can be read independently of other chapters, but the chapters do build on each other. So to get full benefit of the book, I would suggest reading the chapters consecutively. Given the brevity of the book, this should be an easy matter. However, for those who prefer to skim through their books, I would suggest reading the bold-print blurbs that are interspersed throughout the pages. They do not tell the whole story, but they offer insights I think the artist will find valuable and useful.

With technology and the internet expanding and changing so rapidly, I've avoided going into technical discussions in depth. In Appendix IV, there is information on the accompanying website that extends this information.

ABOUT USAGE

The question facing a writer on art and artists is the choice of pronoun to apply to *artist*. There are as many "shes" as there are "hes." With two daughters I am sensitive to gender bias in writing, and using *he* when referring to both men and women does not feel right to me.

I find multiple use of "he or she" as cumbersome. Although the same criticism may be levied against using the construction *s/he*, I find it more acceptable. Critics point to the audible use to s/he, but I am fine with pronouncing this as just *she* .

S/he is a third person singular gender neutral pronoun that takes a singular verb. The plural form of s/he is they, but there is no recognized possessive form for s/he. I choose to use *their*, despite its plural form.

I still use "he or she" when I find its usage to flow better with the text.

It is my hope that the reader will not be so disturbed by this usage that it detracts from the content.

Deciding whether to sell your own work or to pursue galleries is one of the most important decisions the emerging artist will ever make. Reversing that decision in mid-career may not always be possible.

1. Gallery or no gallery?

For artists launching a career in fine art, one of the most important decisions is whether to sell their own work or to seek gallery representation. Twenty years ago, the only realistic path for artists was to seek gallery representation. Today, with the development of the internet and internationalization of the art market, the industry has changed drastically. Because there are so many other art-buying alternatives than galleries, gallery sales have fallen on hard times with a number of commercial galleries declining, especially in non-art destination markets. With the number of commercial galleries declining and the number of artists increasing, the competition for gallery slots has never been so intense.

Selling your own art may not only be viable, but also the best and sometimes the only option for many artists. So what are the advantages and disadvantages of selling your own art versus gallery representation?

The most obvious advantage to selling your own art is that you keep all of the sales. Most galleries charge the artist a 50% commission on their sales. When you include the cost of the frame and materials, there's not much left over for the artist especially when you consider the prices that emerging artists usually get for their work.

Although selling your own art can be a real challenge, you still have greater control over you art life, and do not have to depend on the efforts of others. You also have more creative

control in your painting. You paint what you want to paint
— not what others want you to paint.

Another advantage is that you don't have to spend time
and effort in recruiting galleries. For most artists the process of
seeking galleries is extremely stressful. Placing yourself under
the scrutiny of gallery directors is never pleasant. You also avoid
the problems associated with gallery representation that are
covered later in the chapter.

So what are the disadvantages of selling your own work?

Many artists simply do not possess the interpersonal
and business skills that selling their own art requires. Also,
there must be a substantial investment in time devoted to the
business, which takes away
from painting time. For many
artists, this can be extremely
frustrating and not worth the
effort regardless of personal
sales success.

For most artists, the
process of seeking galleries
is extremely stressful.
Placing yourself under the
scrutiny of gallery directors
is never pleasant.

The artist must also
open up his or her studio to
visitors. I know artists who
hate it when their own spouses enter their studios, so allowing
strangers into your studio, especially if it is in your home, can be
difficult for the artist and the family.

From a financial point of view, there are real limits to
the price that you can sell your work, especially if you are an
emerging artist. And as long as you continue to sell your own
work, those limitations persist. It is very difficult to push up
your prices without losing old collectors. If you choose the
gallery path, your prices will naturally climb as you move up to

better galleries.

Finally, there is the matter of recognition. This is unfortunate, but to be recognized as a significant artist you must be represented by significant galleries. It is the gallery's responsibility to build the artists's reputation through exhibits and promotional efforts. These efforts should enhance the artist's reputation and with it, the prices for the work.

So even though the gallery may be taking 50% of the sales, they are working to raise the artist's prices higher than the artist could do alone. In many cases, when an artist joins a new gallery, the gallery will want to push up the artist's prices, especially in the more established galleries. This is normal. However, if a new gallery suggests lowering prices it is probably not the gallery one should be in. After all, a major reason to seek galleries is to increase prices, not lower them.

To be recognized as a significant artist, you must be represented by significant galleries.

Of course, the most obvious reason to have galleries selling your work is that it should give you more time to paint. However, one should not underestimate the amount of time required in working with a gallery, especially one out of your own market.

So what are the disadvantages of gallery representation? Something that most artists don't think about is that gallery representation can raise your stress level. If you are selling well, they can create stress by demanding more work and perhaps, work of a very specific kind. And if you're not selling, then you are stressed out because you are worried they are going to ask you to leave.

Related to this, is that some artists become intimidated by galleries and become fearful that their work will not be judged strong enough to be shown in the gallery. I knew a very wonderful painter that became so fearful that her work was not up to the standards of her new gallery that she could not produce work for months. Ultimately, she recovered the joy of painting only after she left the gallery.

Galleries want only what they think they can sell. We once represented a painter who painted the most beautiful flower paintings, especially roses. In fact, we had a waiting list of a dozen collectors for his rose paintings. Every time the gallery director had a conversation with the artist, she would always ask when he was going to paint us another rose painting. Now there are some artists who would be happy to spend their lives basically painting the same piece, but for most artists, this would drain them of all of their creativity.

Galleries only want what they think they can sell.

There are additional financial costs associated with gallery representation. The cost of maintaining a framed inventory is a major expense for the artist whereas artists selling out of their own studio will have most of the work unframed. The framing issue really comes to fore in the case of a gallery show. In most cases, the artist is expected to provide twenty or thirty pieces with frames. Depending on the quality of frame, this could represent a substantial investment. With some shows only selling a few paintings, this can become a painful financial experience.

Gallery or no gallery?

We represented a painter on the other side of the country. Both she and we were very excited and optimistic about her show. She was and still is a real talent. She shipped us over forty paintings for the show. When the paintings arrived, many of the frames had split apart, and there was a considerable cost in repairing them.

Then, there were also a full-page ad in a national art magazine and a very nice invitation that we mailed to 2000 collectors. It was our policy to split advertising and invitation costs with our artists.

We sold one small painting in the show. We kept many of the pieces, but still shipped back the majority. We assumed all of the costs of

> **Never do a solo show with a gallery until you have developed a reliable base of collectors with the gallery.**

the invitation, but not the advertising bill. So with her returned paintings, she received a check for the one painting that sold and a bill of over a thousand dollars for her half of the advertising. An art career can be painful!

The other lesson from this is that gallery representation can represent other financial investments as well, such as promotion and advertising. Artists are always excited about the possibility of doing a show. They sometimes overlook the potential costs that a show involves.

A second lesson to take away from this experience is to never do a solo show with a gallery until you have developed a reliable base of collectors with that gallery. Reliability in this case is demonstrated by consistent and significant sales.

Relationships with galleries always evolve into personal

relationships. Like all personal relationships, some are good ones and some are not so good. There are times when the business side of the relationship is successful but the interpersonal side is unpleasant. And similarly, there are times where the interpersonal relationship is wonderful, but the painting sales are woeful. Each of these situations can be emotionally challenging.

Relationships with galleries always evolve into personal relationships. Like all relationships some are good ones, and some are not so good.

Also, there is always the potential for financial problems. Just because a gallery sells your work, it does not always mean you will get your check. As tough as it is to sell work, you don't want to have to chase your money. Chasing money from a gallery can dominate an artist's life and psyche, which really diminishes the enthusiasm to paint art for that gallery and maybe any gallery. All artists have had galleries close on them, which means they had to hunt down their paintings — sometimes successfully, sometimes not.

So what is the right decision for you? If you are not a person who really enjoys the interaction with people, then selling your own art will never work. If you are an artist who is seeking recognition, you will rarely receive that recognition as an artist selling your own work. If you are computer-phobic, you will be significantly handicapped in selling your own work. In each of these cases, you are better off finding galleries to represent you.

Almost every artist, even those represented by prominent

national galleries, sell work out of their studios. This is the natural evolution of an art career. Collectors will find the artist. But for the emerging artist, finding time to pursue galleries and selling their own work and still having time to paint can be difficult. Under certain conditions, an artist may consider a business model of selling their paintings in their local market and recruit galleries out of market.

Chasing money from a gallery can dominate an artist's life and psyche, which really diminishes the enthusiasm to paint for that gallery and maybe any gallery

This plan works best for the artist who maintains a studio outside the home where they can show and sell their work. This is especially true in a multi-studio situation where there are opportunities to do cooperative marketing and sales activities with other artists.

The answer, gallery or no gallery? The artist should do a self-audit of his or her own personality and skills to answer that question. However, this book is directed to artists who have decided to pursue galleries.

Most artists believe that talent is the only criteria for a successful art career. There are some very talented artists who have failed, while some not so very talented artists have succeeded.

2. Are you ready?

One of the most important questions for emerging artists is whether they are ready to make the move to a professional art career. There is a sense that there is a magical level of ability that will translate immediately into success. Certainly, ability plays a part in the success of an artist, but ability is not sufficient in ensuring sales. There are many technically talented artists who do not sell their art.

In selling art, the most important quality is what I call *collector resonance*. Collector resonance is what resonates with the collectors and compels them to purchase the art. There are many factors that determine this resonance. Of course, technical excellence is one of those factors, but subject matter, narrative and even the choice of colors will play a part. Defining collector resonance is difficult, but for the seasoned art professional, the quality is always clearly apparent.

Unfortunately, collector resonance is not something that can be learned like other technical qualities. Artists must paint those things they love to paint in the manner in which they feel they should be painted. Fortunately for some artists, what they like to paint is what collectors like to buy. Artists, who try to alter their style and paint for collectors, discover it usually does not work, because the artist has lost the joy of painting. And that joy of painting is an important component of collector resonance.

So when is an artist ready to approach galleries and launch

a professional art career? It is when the artist has reached a level of technical competence to paint his or her vision. This simply means that the artist can competently paint what they wish to paint. That does not mean the artist has the ability to paint every scene or idea, but that s/he has the competence to paint their vision."

This also implies the artist has reached a stage in which they know basically what they want to paint. If the artist is still experimenting with different styles and subject matters, it is a pretty good probability that he or she is not ready to launch an art career. This is not to say the artist must stop evolving as an artist, but that the core essence of the art has been established. From this core, the artist can evolve slowly and thoughtfully. Great art only occurs when the artist pushes to be a greater artist.

Galleries are usually not interested in artists who have no artistic core.

Galleries are usually not interested in artists who have no artistic core. For once they have developed a market for the artist's work, they don't want to jeopardize that market by work that is dramatically different from the style that initially attracted collector enthusiasm and interest. Individuals collect art because the art resonates with them and that it possesses attributes they find pictorially appealing. When an artist departs from these attributes, the collectors depart as well.

So how much change will collectors accept in an artist's work? Collectors and their galleries will accept evolution in the artist's work so long as they can still recognize the work as the artist's. If the work becomes profoundly new, then the work might as well be of that of a new artist.

History is full of great artists who evolved profoundly throughout their careers — Picasso, Cézanne and Matisse are good examples. However, this does not mean that when they made their artistic shifts that collectors immediately accepted the new art.

So the lesson for the artist is that you better enjoy creating the kind of paintings you are presenting to galleries, because if you succeed, it will be hard to move from that style and subject matter.

There are also practical matters that an artist must consider before launching a professional art career. The artist must have the time to devote to painting. Artist needs to be able to paint at least 20 hours a week, and probably more. So having a full time job and attempting a painting career only works if the artist is willing to sacrifice everything else in life.

Artists require economic resources for a myriad of expenses beyond the basics of art supplies and frames. And if the plan is to paint full time, then there must be money for living expenses. There are a few artists who sell immediately, but they are rare, and it normally takes several years for an artist to become even moderately successful. If an artist does not possess these resources, mounting stresses can quickly compromise the joy of painting.

Not only does the artist need time to paint, but there must also be time to do the business of art. Buying supplies, securing frames and shipping artwork are all time-consuming as well as money-consuming activities.

There is also the issue of inventory. Every new gallery

will want to have at least ten strong paintings with frames. If an artist does not have an inventory of strong paintings, they should postpone their gallery search until they do. Only artists with reputation can sell their ordinary work. For the emerging artist, the standard is much higher.

Finally, there is the cost of failure. Many artists fail because they launch their careers prematurely, and some never recover from the experience. There are few enterprises more difficult than establishing a fine art career. Most do not succeed, and if you are not really ready, then there is little chance of success.

3. Requisites for the artist

Whether you are planning to work primarily with galleries or selling your own art, there are certain necessary requisites and skills that every artist should have. Without these requisites and skills, the artist will find it difficult to do business.

Business Cards

Even the most novice artist usually has business cards. S/he may not always carry them, but most artists recognize the importance of an attractive business card. The standard white or beige card with text will not suffice, and most artists have cards with an image of one of their paintings.

The business card is usually the first communication the artist has with a gallery or a collector, so the painting on the card should reflect the artist's best work in their dominant subject matter. If you paint primarily landscapes, you don't want to pass out cards with a portrait image.

Because you want to expose your art to the recipient, the card should include an internet address where the person can see more of your work. This may be your own website or one of the many free sites an artist can utilize to show their work. Wherever the website, it should have an easy-to-find email link so potential collectors and galleries can contact you. Along with the web site address, the card should also have your email address.

Although email has become the predominant form of communication, there are people who might want to talk to you in person, so the card should also include your telephone number. If you include your postal mailing address, you are going to find yourself on a multitude of mailing lists. This includes mailings from galleries, and since an important process in recruiting galleries is gallery research, these mailings can even be helpful. For instance, a gallery might announce an exhibition of a new artist. The fact that a gallery has taken on a new artist is valuable information in itself along with the kind of artist they have added.

With all of this information, an artist business card will have to be two sided or a folded business card. Twenty years ago, a two-sided card with a full color image could cost a couple hundred dollars. Today, with digital printing, the cost will be a small fraction of that.

Digital Camera

Of all of the recent technological innovations, none has saved the artist more money than the development of digital cameras. Photography used to be a great expense for artist with the cost of film and processing. Slides were required with every submitted gallery portfolio. And if you needed to have an image reproduced for prints or for advertising, there was the expense of hiring a photographer to shoot 4 x 5" negatives or positives. Digital cameras have changed all of that.

A 16-gigabyte memory disk can hold hundreds of high-resolution pictures. So instead of packing twenty rolls of film for a trip, the artist only needs a single memory disk the size of a small matchbook. Although some gallery directors still request slides with submitted portfolios, it is becoming a rarer request. Even in these cases, quality and reasonably priced slides can be developed from digital images. Nor do most juried shows request slides any more and an artist's images can be uploaded to national online application providers where the same set of images can be reused for multiple juried submissions.

Resolution for digital cameras has increased dramatically

since they were first introduced. Digital cameras selling for under $200 now offer enough resolution to print high-quality reproductions and advertisements. Before digital technology, the artist had to rely on the ability of the printer in creating accurate color presentation. Often the results were atrocious. Now when we send images to the printer or magazine, we can preview the images securely, and be assured the color will be what we want.

Unfortunately, most artists don't realize the potential of their digital camera. This is particularly the case when photographing their own art. The problem is how few artists actually read their manuals where they can learn the rules of "white balance." White balance settings adjust the camera's interpretation of light under different conditions. Without making these adjustments, images will rarely match the true color of the work.

Artists should choose a camera that allows for manual white balance settings. Because of their software, some cameras are much better at color adjustment than others. Most artists are oversold on resolution whereas the camera's software interpretation of color is more important. There is no shortage of digital camera reviews on the web, and the artist would be wise to check these out before putting out three hundred dollars for a camera that may not accurately record color.

Computer

Not to overstate the obvious, the artist should have a personal computer, either a laptop or a tabletop, and know how to use it. With the development of smart phones and tablets, many artists have moved away from the personal computer. This is a mistake. A successful career in the fine art business requires a computer. You need the power of a personal computer to edit and maintain the images of your paintings. Tablets and ibooks offer email capacity, but they do not usually provide the power of a full-fledged email program.

Important business software includes a database, preferably one that will allow you to store images and a personal finance program. I know these involve an investment in time and money, but you can't underestimate the value of organization. Galleries who are organized appreciate artists who are as well. Artists need to know where their paintings are located, and the moneys due from sales. Any artist that expects their galleries to do this is asking for trouble.

Email

Having an email address is as important as having a mailing address, and artists should consider having two — one for their personal correspondence and one for their arts-related correspondence. To receive and send email, there are two types of clients (software applications). First, there are the computer-based programs that you set up on your own computer where they can only be accessed. Thunderbird and Outlook are examples of these types of programs. The second are web-based programs that can be accessed wherever there is internet access. These programs are usually tied in with browser programs such as Google (Gmail) and Yahoo (Yahoo Mail).

Each of these email solutions has their advantages and disadvantages. Computer email programs offer more features such as powerful address books that facilitate email promotion. Plus, your email address should be associated with your website, e.g. "myname@www.mywebsite.com." So anyone who knows your email will also know where to see your art.

On the negative side, they are more difficult to set up and learn, and you cannot access your email easily when on the road.

Web based solutions are simple to set up and you can easily access your email wherever you're traveling. However, they lack many of the features of a computer-based email program, and you are subject to viewing advertisements with every email.

One consideration the artist needs to know if they are using a computer-based program: a computer-based program requires an email server account, which is usually included with your internet access account. Some providers have significant limits on the size of attachments that can be sent or received with an email. Artists are always required to send high-resolution files that could surpass the limits allowed by their mail server provider while most of the web-based solutions have very high attachment limits.

In the beginning of World Wide Web, artist sites were luxury — today they are a necessity.

Because of their marketing potential, a computer-based email solution is the best choice for your art-related email address, while a web-based solution, such as Gmail, can be used for your personal emails.

Website

In the beginning of the World Wide Web, artist sites were a luxury — today they are a necessity. For the artists selling their own work, the website is an essential component of sales process, and for artists seeking galleries, it is a crucial exposure tool. The business of art demands that artists have exposure on the web — preferably with their own site.

Technology for building websites has evolved to a point where even the most technically-challenged can develop their own site. For those who are still intimidated by the prospect, there are companies that will provide a site for a moderate monthly fee. Some of these companies also provide some promotional services, but these services rarely create sales. For the artist who doesn't have a budget for a website, there are many free alternatives.·

For artists whose primary website purpose is to expose their art to galleries, their websites requires little complexity — a few gallery pages, a bio and some contact links are all that is really needed. For the artist, who is attempting to sell off the website, the project can be much more difficult and may require the services of a professional web designer.

The decision of having a professional design and maintain a website depend on the artist's own ability and personal resources. The expertise required to build a website is not nearly as difficult when early designers had to code their sites by hand. Today, programs have simplified the process, but for some, it is still a challenge. For these artists, hiring a specialist or contracting with one of

If an artist expects significant art sales from their website, he or she will be disappointed.

the many companies that provide ready-made sites, makes sense. However, even when a website is contracted, there is an expenditure of time that is required to get the information and images to the designer. Communication between the artist and designer may not always be perfect, and there are cases when an artist can spend as much time talking to the designer as it would have taken he or she to complete the work. Of course for artists does not have the resources to pay someone else, they must learn to do their own site.

If an artist expects significant art sales from their website, he or she will be disappointed. The website is an effective tool to assist in the selling process. Generally, no collector purchases a piece of art from a website unless they have already seen the artist's work in person, and even in these cases they still want to speak to the artist before sending a check.

The big three in social media for the artist are Facebook, Google+ and LinkedIn. Facebook is the only option that is almost mandatory, and is probably as important to artists as their website.

Regardless of your purpose in setting up your website, you should make it easy for the visitor to contact you. Many sites include an email response form instead of an email address. This is protection against email gleaners who sell their lists to spammers. No one likes their email to be jammed with spam, but if the email form demands too much information from the sender, they won't bother. If you don't include a phone number, you won't get a call, and many art sales begin with a telephone call.

Once you have set up your site, every piece of your printed and online materials should include your website address (URL). This includes your email, especially if your email address is different from your web address.

Social Media Presence

There are hundreds of sites on the internet that could be defined as social media and dozens of these are art-related. So if the artist were inclined, s/he could spend hours establishing and maintaining presence on these sites. Fortunately, for the artist there are only three sites that are probably worth the effort: Facebook, Google+ and LinkedIn. Of course, the internet is always rapidly changing and in a few years new opportunities may emerge. Of these three, Facebook is the only option that is almost mandatory. Social media is discussed in more depth in chapter five, "Art is a People Business."

Portfolio

Even in this age of digital images, an artist who is actively pursuing galleries needs a pictorial portfolio for in-person presentations. Twenty years ago gallery directors would use a slide-viewer or a light table to preview an artist's slides. Most of today's gallery directors probably don't even own a slide-viewer or a light table.

When sending a portfolio, a CD is the accepted and desirable choice. For the artist, it is a cost efficient way to present their work. A slide and printed portfolio could cost the artist ten to twenty dollars to produce and several dollars to ship. And there was a very good chance it would never be returned. A CD is about a dollar to produce and ship.

The CD is also more convenient for the gallery directors, who are not obliged to return it, and the individual can examine the work at their own leisure, and retain a pictorial record of the artist's work.

However, when sitting down with the gallery director, a portfolio of large images in a binder is a more effective tool.

There is something more personal with an album that is missing when viewing the work on a computer screen. The computer becomes a device that separates the artist from the gallery director. If they are using the artist's laptop or tablet, the gallery director has lost control of the presentation since they must depend on the artist to scroll through the work. And if the presentation must be viewed on the gallery computer, the director may feel the artist has usurped their computer.

Even in this age of digital media, an artist who is actively pursuing galleries needs a pictorial portfolio, for not every gallery has embraced the digital revolution

The old-fashioned album allows the director to view the work as they wish and facilitates conversation and discussion about the work. Plus, paintings presented on paper provide the gallery director with a more realistic view of the work. After the interview, the artist can leave a CD which the gallery director can review.

Such a portfolio may have been cost-prohibitive before digital technology, but today's inkjet printers can produce letter sized reproductions for under a dollar a sheet. And the quality and the fidelity of the images can equal or even surpass traditional photographic prints. However, to produce such images requires a decent digital camera and quality inkjet printer.

Mini-Portfolio

When I give my workshop, *The Artist in Search of a Gallery*, I tell the participants the following suggestion will be worth the $95 they invested in the workshop. This is the mini-portfolio. The mini-portfolio is a miniature of the larger portfolio. Instead of a portfolio of 8 x 10" pictures, it is a portfolio of 4 x 6" pictures or similar size. You should produce your own personal mini-portfolio in a nice leather album and a few others in cheaper plastic albums that can be given away. The album should hold between 16 and 24 pictures, and every page should be filled. (Unfilled pages give the impression you have not painted enough pieces to fill the album.) Again, using an inkjet printer and inexpensive pocket albums, the cost is only a couple dollars per mini-portfolio.

And most important of all, you should have the album with you wherever you go. The mini-portfolio will not do you much good unless you always have it with you. If the artist will carry it everywhere, I can almost guarantee that they will generate additional sales.

The mini-portfolio is a great selling tool. All artists have had the question directed to them, "What kind of art do you do?" In fact, that is almost the inevitable question when you introduce yourself as an artist. Instead of trying to grapple with words to describe your art, the mini-portfolio answers the question for you. Most people are actually interested in seeing the kind of art you do, and if they aren't, they should not have asked the question.

Artists who carry their mini-porfolio with them all the time will sell at least one painting a year that they would not have sold.

I know some artists put images of their paintings on their smartphones and tablets, but psychologically, it is much less aggressive handing a person the mini-portfolio than forcing them to share your technology. This is particularly true for older generations.

Many of those who have taken my workshop have told me later that the mini-portfolio has generated sales for them. One artist returned the week after the workshop to tell me she had already sold two paintings from her mini-portfolio!

The cheaper mini-portfolios come in handy when visiting galleries. Often your conversations will be with a salesperson or an assistant director, who may react positively to your work, and want to show it to the gallery director or owner. Leaving your business card will probably not result any positive action, but the mini-portfolio may. Regardless of the outcome, for investment of only a few dollars, having a portfolio of your work floating around a gallery is never a bad thing.

The personal greeting card

One of the most effective promotional tools for the artist is the personal greeting card. This is the card that the artist uses in written communication to friends, collectors and galleries. Like any greeting card, the front has an image of one the artist's most compelling pieces. The inside is blank to write personal messages, and the backside identifies the art by title with the artist's name and web address.

One of the most effective promotional tools for the artist is the personal greeting card.

In my gallery, I developed a personal greeting card for each of my artists, and I would use it to thank collectors for visiting the gallery. If the collector expressed a particular interest in an artist, I would select that artist's greeting card. If the collector were interested in a particular painting, I would create a card with that painting on the front. There were several sales that would not have happened if I had not followed up and sent the card. One collector told me, she put the card on her refrigerator for six months, and one day decided she just had to have the painting.

With today's computer applications and a decent inkjet printer, creating such cards does not require extensive design and computer skills. For those who are computer-challenged, cards can be ordered online for under a dollar a card.

The personal greeting card is an important tool in recruiting out-of-market galleries. It serves as the follow-up vehicle after visiting prospective galleries. Artist postcards are often discarded before they ever reach the targeted decision-maker in the gallery. Whereas a hand-addressed greeting card envelope will nearly always reach the person to whom it is addressed. It also has a much greater impact on the recipient than any email message. The greeting card expresses to the receiver that you find them important and significant. People like to buy paintings from artists they like.

Inventory of framed paintings

There is no sense to pursue galleries if you do not have the inventory to support your gallery. If you succeed in recruiting a gallery, they will require an immediate inventory of work. For every piece that is displayed in a gallery, they want to have at least two more in inventory. So a new gallery will require an inventory of about ten pieces. It is important not only to have this many framed pieces, but they also should be strong pieces.

An artist's success in a new gallery depends heavily on his or her sales during the first three months. If the quality of the initial body of work does not generate those sales, the gallery will lose its enthusiasm for the artist, and all of the pieces end up in the storage room. So if you don't have ten strong pieces to send to your gallery, you are better off waiting until you do.

I recognize this requisite list may seem like overkill to many artists, but not doing business in the right way is the path to failure, and there is no business more subject to failure than the business of art.

No matter what they claim, all galleries are always seeking new artists. What they are not interesting in is interviewing new artists.

4. What are galleries looking for anyway?

No matter what they claim, all galleries are always seeking new artists. This does not mean to say they are publicizing this truth, and, in fact, most galleries want to conceal this reality, because they do not want to invest the time in interviewing prospective artists. This is why a great percentage of galleries will tell inquiring artists that their gallery is not currently seeking new artists. So what are galleries looking for anyway?

The 20/80 rule

In every sales organization, there is something called the 20/80 rule. This rule states that twenty percent of the salesmen make eighty percent of the sales. This rule also applies to galleries where twenty percent of the artists sell eighty percent of the work. Galleries are always seeking these 20/80 artists.

This 20/80 rule applies to both number of sales and the sales volume in dollars. A major artist, selling work at substantial prices, may not be selling many pieces, but his or her sales volume is high. Conversely, a popular emerging artist may generate numerous sales without high dollar volume. Although galleries have a preference for major artists selling for high prices, they are also seeking artists who generate sales volume. Sales, regardless of price, create excitement in the gallery.

There are only a few of these 20/80 artists and they are usually fairly well established. Whenever these artists are available, galleries snatch them up. For these artists, this book has little relevance.

Prestige artists

Galleries are always seeking artists that will elevate the prestige of the gallery. They will seek these artists even when the artist does not sell well. There is always the presumption that prestigious artists sell, but that is not always the case. Adding such artists imparts celebrity to the gallery, and this celebrity helps the gallery attract other artists who do sell. Ascending artists always seek to show in galleries whose roster includes prestigious artists.

Artists to fill gallery holes

Most successful galleries have a recognizable envelope of art. But within this envelope there are holes. These holes may be a matter of style, subject matter or price point. Astute gallery managers are aware of these holes and are always looking for artists to fill these holes.

I believe that to paint compelling art, the artist should be compelled by the subject matter. Nevertheless, I have known artists who possessed the ability to paint appealing work even when they were not enamoured with the subject matter.

In the 1990's, a New York artist became very popular with his paintings of frenetic women in interesting urban settings. He painted these women in a very distinctive and appealing style. The paintings caught the attention of gallery owners who sought to add the artist to their galleries. When they could not secure the original artist, they turned to the dozens of other artists who emulated his style. Since he was a very popular teacher as well, there was no shortage of artists to fill the void.

Certain subject matters can also become popular. Farm animals were not exactly a hot-selling subject until a West Coast artist began painting them in bright expressionist colors. Again, galleries began looking around for artists who could emulate the artist's farm animals. Suddenly, there was regiment of Expressionist artists painting cows and roosters.

I believe that to paint compelling art, the artist should be compelled by the subject matter. I have known artists who possessed the ability to paint appealing work even when they were not necessarily enamored with the subject matter.

A final example pertains to a New Mexico gallery, who had a stable of first rank artists. What the gallery did not have was a reasonably priced landscape painter, who could paint Southwestern scenes in compelling way. Although he considered it unlikely that his work would be accepted by the gallery, the artist presented his work. The gallery director was impressed with his landscapes, which

There are some gallery directors who view themselves as cultivators of fresh talent. As rare as these people are, they can be instrumental in developing an artist's career.

filled the hole in the gallery. And he quickly became one of the gallery's most popular selling artists.

For the emerging artist, there are opportunities in even significant galleries if they can find a hole in the gallery's stable of artists. The key is to identify these opportunities and to effectively present art that can fill those holes.

Developmental artists

There are a few galleries that actually seek artists whom

they believe have the potential to become significant. This is more of a romantic notion as opposed to a realistic one, but it does happen. There are some gallery directors and owners who view themselves as cultivators of fresh talent. As rare as these people are, they can be instrumental in developing an artist's career.

It is not always easy to spot such galleries. In most cases, these gallery directors would even deny they are seeking artists to develop, but they are open to representing an emerging artist when they see one whose work evokes their interest.

There is no easy way to find such gallery advocates. General advice is just to be seen in as many places as possible, and especially places where gallery directors and managers may be present. Although jury fees for major exhibitions may be high, such exhibitions usually attract these kinds of people. Although a local juried gallery show is probably not going to draw a great deal of attention from other gallery directors, it will place your work before the gallery's own director, who may see sales potential in your work.

Start-up galleries

For emerging artists, new galleries are always the easiest to find representation. However, it is a dangerous proposition because of the high failure rate of new galleries. But there are new galleries that do succeed, and have helped launch the careers of many artists. Notwithstanding the dangers involved with a start-up gallery, more people will see your artwork there than in your home studio.

Final piece of advice: always give your new gallery your best work, but never risk a major portion of your inventory with one gallery, especially a new one.

5. Art is a people business

The art business is very much a people business. If a gallery director does not like you, there's little chance you will find representation with that gallery regardless of the quality of your work. As a part of your gallery research, you should investigate the human energy of every prospective gallery. If you don't feel comfortable with the gallery staff and how they treat customers and artists, that gallery is probably not a good fit for your art and your life. The art business is a hard business, and it becomes even harder if you are around people whom you don't respect and who don't respect you. You should not have to try to make the gallery staff like you. The best relationships are ones that are naturally and honestly developed.

When you visit prospective galleries, you should register in their guest books. If there is a comments section, you should comment on the art and perhaps specific artists. Galleries sometimes use these comments to determine whether they place individuals on their mailing list. Once you begin to receive mail and emails pertaining to their events, you should make it a goal to attend as many of these events as possible. The objective is to become a recognizable person in the gallery, and one who is liked. One word of caution: unless you actually plan to purchase a painting at an opening, conversation with the staff should be at a minimum for their attention is primarily on selling, not with socializing with other artists.

You should also visit their website and Facebook page. If

they offer an eletter on their website, you should also sign up for it as well. And in the case of Facebook, by choosing "like" you will receive their posts, and if the gallery has a "follow" link that will also put you on their posting list.

Networking

Most artists do not fully understand the value of networking in recruiting galleries to represent their work. And even among those who do recognize this importance, many are reluctant to utilize networking connections. Artists, who fail to use these resources, place themselves at a significant disadvantage compared to artists who do. The notion of competition is distasteful for many artists, but the reality is that artists have to compete for collectors and galleries. There are only so many gallery slots open to artists, and the artists who gain these slots are not always the most creative and talented.

Most artists do not fully understand the value of networking in recruiting galleries, and even among those who do recognize this importance, many are reluctant to utilize networking connections.

As it has been noted previously, the essential objective of the artist is to have an opportunity to have their artwork reviewed by the gallery director or whoever make the artist decisions for the gallery. So the networking efforts are directed toward that goal.

The initial and essential information for the aspiring artist is to find out who makes that decision for the gallery. In the majority of the cases, that person will be the gallery director, but often a gallery owner may have input or even final say on new artists. Finding out who is the gallery director is as easy as picking up a business card, but discovering the gallery recruitment procedures are not always as evident. The easiest way is to simply ask one of the gallery artists. The galleries themselves often obfuscate this information.

Once you know who the decision-maker is, your next task is to find someone who may know this person, and hopefully, carries some weight with the decision-maker. This is usually one of three groups of people. First, and the easiest to discover, are the artists who show in the gallery. If you are friendly with one of the artists, you can ask if s/he will give you a referral. If the artist is confident and comfortable with their position in the gallery, s/he may be glad to give you a recommendation.

There are only so many gallery slots open to artists, and the artists that gain these slots are not always the most creative and talented.

Remember, you are not asking the artist to recommend you to the gallery, but only to recommend the gallery director to take a look at your work. This may be a subtle distinction, but it's one that makes the request much more palatable to both you and the recommending artist.

The power of an artist's referral depends on the status of the artist in the gallery. If the artist is a major artist or *the* major artist, the referral holds much greater weight than if the artist is a minor artist. An enthusiastic recommendation from a gallery's major artist may often be sufficient to warrant a gallery invitation.

In my first gallery, we represented an artist who accounted

for about half of our dollar sales volume. He recommended an artist that neither myself nor the gallery owner felt would be a good fit for the gallery. Nevertheless, the invitation to join the gallery was extended without even a formal review. The artist did not sell a single painting is the three years he was with the gallery, but the owner did not want to risk alienating the major artist who recommended him.

Whenever you take a workshop, it is a good policy to investigate the galleries in which the workshop-giver shows. For in the course of the workshop, the artist who is presenting the workshop may offer praise on your work. If the praise appears to be honest, you may ask for a gallery referral. Again, the request is not a recommendation for representation, but just for the opportunity for the gallery director to critique the artist's work. The word *critique* is much less threatening than *review*. Review implies a formal presentation, which also implies some decision. People rarely want to be placed in a position to make decisions, especially negative ones.

Friendships between artists can be fragile things. Having a friend refuse to recommend you to a gallery is going to jeopardize the friendship.

I should issue a word of caution. Friendships between artists can be fragile things. Whenever you ask any favor, the request may not be well received. Because of artistic egos, friendships have been lost simply based on an unflattering comment about a painting. Having a friend refuse to recommend you to a gallery, for whatever reason, is certainly going to jeopardize the friendship.

Gallery people respect what other gallery people have to say. When artists tell a gallery that they sell very well, the gallery people take that information with a large grain of salt. No gallery director has ever heard a prospective artist claim he or she didn't sell very well.

Conversely, when a gallery tells another gallery that a particular artist is one of their best selling, the recommendation carries a lot of weight. Why would one gallery recommend an artist to another gallery? First, gallery people have friends in other galleries, and if the other gallery is not geographically competitive, the recommendation can be viewed as a favor to both the artist and the other gallery.

Although galleries are protective of their artists, they also develop friendships with these artists, and want them to succeed — even if it means allowing another gallery to participate in that success.

In one of my galleries, we had a very good relationship with a prominent West Coast gallery. The result of that relationship was that we "traded" a few artists. That is, we took on some of their artists, with their blessing, and they took on some of ours.

Recommendations from former gallery associates can also be influential. Although an artist's current gallery may be reluctant to refer an artist to another gallery, there is little reluctance for individuals who have left the gallery business. This includes sales people who have sold your work.

A final group of individuals who also have influence with galleries are collectors — especially active and significant collectors. One of our best collectors spent half a year in our city and half the year in a resort city in western Florida. He took it on his own initiative to recommend one of our artists to the major gallery in the city. Based on that recommendation, the artist was asked to join their gallery, which was the beginning of a very beneficial relationship. Our gallery director was not particularly pleased about this, but wasn't going to do anything that would jeopardize the relationship with either the collector or the artist.

I have known artists who have asked collector friends to scope out galleries when they take trips. It never hurts artists when collectors extol their virtues to other galleries.

Social media

In terms of human networking for the artist, you cannot underestimate the importance of social media. There are hundreds of social media sites on the web with some that are directed specifically to artists. However, the only site that really matters is Facebook. With almost a billion members and growing, Facebook dwarfs all other social media, including Google+. For the artist, who doesn't want to spend hours learning the intricacies of many sites, this is fortuitous. Unfortunately, Facebook is not always the most intuitive of sites to learn, and this is aggravated by their continuous tinkering with its features. Maybe in the future, there will be an easier and more effective alternative, but that is not the case today. Thus, if you're an artist, you cannot afford not to have a Facebook page, and a minimum of knowledge on how to use it.

Gallery directors have gravitated to Facebook, because they want see what their artists are doing and creating.

Facebook places a high priority on pictures and video,

which for the visual artist is an ideal medium. In the simplest of terms, the more people who see your art, the more sales that are going to result.

For the artist seeking gallery representation, Facebook can be a valuable tool. Recruiting galleries is also about getting your work before gallery directors and owners. You may not have many Facebook friends who own and manage galleries, but some of your friends may — especially among your art friends.

Gallery directors have gravitated to Facebook, because they want to see what their artists are doing and creating. Galleries are always hoping to get the best work from their artists. In the earlier days of the internet, we would regularly visit other gallery websites who represented some of our artists. It was always disturbing to discover a great painting that went to another gallery. Since most artists post their new paintings on their Facebook page, it is a convenient way for galleries to keep tabs on their artists.

So when an artist posts a new painting, there is always the potential that picture can find its way to a gallery director's Facebook page. All it takes is one compelling image to get a gallery invite.

Facebook is also a powerful researching tool. Knowing what's happening with other artists is very helpful information. Artists will normally post information regarding gallery events and any new galleries that are representing their work. When an artist joins a new gallery, it is evident that the gallery is open to new artists, and such a gallery might be receptive to other new artists.

Another way to keep current with galleries is to "follow" (become a Facebook follower) galleries in which you are interested. By checking the "Like" button you become a follower. By being a follower, you will receive their posts that may also provide some valuable information such as juried shows, new artists and perhaps their guidelines for artist applications.

Artists can be even more aggressive with their Facebook page. You may post, "I would love to show in Sedona. Does anyone know of galleries who are looking for new artists? I think (the picture of the posted painting) this desert landscape would be well received there."

For some artists with a large national following, they can set up a page as an artist page, which is separate from a personal page. These can be particularly effective for artists who regularly give workshops, etc. For most artists, the additional page is probably not worth the effort, especially if the artist also maintains a website.

Regardless whether you are an emerging artist or a nationally acclaimed one, a Facebook page is almost as important as your website.

Although there are dangers involved when exploiting your network of friends and artists, an artist should not ignore net-working as important tool in every aspect of the business of art, including the gallery search.

6. Getting inside the gallery director's mind

When a gallery director sees the work of an emerging artist, there are three primary factors that influence his or her response.

First, does the gallery director personally like the work? There are many factors that go into "liking." Some gallery directors have preferences for specific styles and genres. Since gallery directors spend all day with their art, it's natural that they would prefer to be around artwork, that they enjoy.

Secondly, does the gallery director find the work up to the standards of the gallery? Most gallery directors prize excellence in the technical work of a painting. The word "painterly" means different things to different people. Regardless of how they define painterly, most gallery directors seek that quality in the work they sell.

Thirdly, does the gallery director believe s/he can sell the work? Regardless of how wonderful the gallery director may think of the art, if s/he does not think the gallery can sell the work, it is unlikely the gallery will represent the artist. After all, the only way a gallery can stay in business is through art sales.

Not only does every gallery have its own artistic personality but also a collector personality. The savvy gallery director knows what their collectors buy, and strives to present art that appeals to these preferences. Not all collectors have great taste, but the gallery director must offer a body of work that serves these tastes. Thus, a gallery director may appreciate an artist's work, but still reject it because they feel their collectors will not respond positively.

A related factor is that the gallery director may not think that the artwork will sell because of the price. Most galleries offer a distinctive envelope of art within a set range of prices for that art. Thus, if the artist's prices fall out of that range the gallery will be reluctant to accept the artist. If the gallery cannot sell work for more than a thousand dollars, then it is fruitless to take on an artist whose work sells for much more. Conversely, if the artist's work sells below the gallery's price range, they will probably pass on the artist. In some cases, the gallery will suggest the artist raise prices. For the emerging artist without galleries, this is an appealing proposition, but for the established artist, raising prices may jeopardize sales in other galleries.

Gallery directors are always cognizant of the opinions of their artists, especially their major artists. This cognizance is well founded for most every gallery has lost significant artists when they have added artists who do not match the credentials and dispositions of their major artists.

An important factor in the gallery's decision is whether the artist fills a perceived need in the gallery. For instance, the gallery may not have a landscape painter whose paintings sell in the lower price range of the gallery. If an artist's work fulfills that need there is a good chance they will recruit the artist.

There are personality factors also that come into play. Gallery directors are much more likely to take on a new artist if they personally like the artist. Gallery directors shy away from artists who have reputations for being "difficult." They may accept such an artist if he or she is well established with collectors, but rarely for an emerging artist. Two of the qualities that most gallery directors hate are arrogance and pushiness. Again, they may overlook arrogance in an artist whose arrogance has some legitimacy, but not for an upstart.

Gallery directors are always cognizant of the opinions of their artists, especially their major artists. This cognizance is well founded for most every gallery has lost significant artists when they have added artists who do not match the credentials and dispositions of their major artists. In fact, many gallery directors will consult with their major artists before they take on a new artist. This is why a prospective artist has a much better chance getting into a gallery if they are recommended by one of the gallery's major artists.

In the art business as in life, if you are going to succeed you need to understand the motivations of others, and accept that these motivations might not match your own. In dealing with gallery directors, understanding their motivations will certainly facilitate successful relationships.

Researching galleries takes time, but in the long run, it saves the artist time and perhaps some embarrassment.

7. Researching galleries

There are two very different strategies in approaching galleries to represent your work. First, there is the scatter-gun approach where the artist contacts galleries almost indiscriminately with the philosophy that if you ask enough times somebody will eventually say "yes." A second strategy is a selective approach where the artist targets a few galleries and directs the attention only to those galleries. The scatter-gun approach does not require a great deal of research, whereas the selective approach does.

The initial research is to determine whether the gallery would be interested in your work. Artists will often misjudge the best candidates for their work. One of the most frequent misjudgments occurs when an artist discovers a gallery which represents an artist who paints just like him or her. You may conclude if a gallery represents John Doe, whose paintings look just like mine (and mine might even be better), then surely they will be interested in me. They probably are not going to be interested in your work, because they already have someone who paints like you. Why would they be interested in another you?

Every rule has its exceptions. There are galleries who show a very tight envelope of artistic style and subjects. If you find such a gallery that shows five artists who paint like you, then it's a pretty good chance they'll be in the market for a sixth.

A variant of this mind-set is the case where you paint

similarly to the gallery's most popular and most successful artist. The artist reasons that since not all collectors can afford the top guy, the gallery will be happy to have someone who is almost as good, but not nearly as expensive. That's as irrational as the first scenario. Why would the gallery want to sell cheaper paintings? Plus, there's a good chance the gallery's prime artist is not going to be pleased to see the gallery carrying a look-a-like who is selling for half the price.

The best possible scenario is one in which your general painting style is consistent with other artists in the gallery, but what you paint is not being represented in the gallery.

We once represented a painter who had the uncanny ability to paint like a famous New England Impressionist. This artist was terribly uncreative, but was a great mimic. We had already approached the master artist, but he was moving out of galleries to open his own.

If we couldn't get the original master, we thought we could recruit an imitator. The mimic's paintings were actually quite beautiful, and everyone commented how much they reminded them of the famous Impressionist's work. Although they were great bargains, we never sold a single painting. Our collectors were just not interested in imitations.

There are times, however, when style and subject matter becomes almost as important as the artist who is most recognized for a certain style of work. Galleries may overlook the emulative qualities of the art if they feel a strong need to show that kind of art. Even in these cases, they prefer work that has some distinctiveness in style.

The best probable scenario is one in which your general painting style is consistent with the other artists in the gallery, but what you paint is not being represented in the gallery. Galleries are always looking for artists who broaden their appeal to collectors.

With the emergence of the internet, researching galleries has never been easier. Simply type in the name of any city followed by *galleries*, and you'll get a fairly large sample of galleries in that city. So if you're planning an art trip, the first place to start is with the internet. An evening on the computer should give you a pretty good idea of prospective galleries.

If you are computer-phobic and have resisted social media, you are at a severe disadvantage as a professional artist. These tools are especially effective research tools for the emerging artists. If you have already established a network of galleries, you can survive without Facebook, but for the emerging artist maintaining social media presence has become a virtual necessity.

A gallery relationship is one of both business and of personality. For the relationship to work, it must work on both the business and interpersonal level.

The next step is to actually visit the galleries. The goal here is not only to investigate the art, but also to get a feel for the people who run the galleries. A gallery relationship is one of business and personality. For the relationship to work, it must work on both the business and interpersonal levels. If you feel comfortable with the staff and you believe your art would work in the gallery, then the next step is to contact the gallery.

The initial research is to determine which galleries may be receptive to you and your work. Once a gallery has shown interest in you, the next research is to determine whether you really want to show in that gallery. For an artist without any gallery representation, securing that first gallery is crucial, for finding additional galleries is much easier when you are showing in at least one gallery. Having said that, it is still important to research every aspect of a prospective gallery you are considering. There are instances where you may be better off waiting for the right gallery opportunity. Before you jump, it is always wise to know where you are going to land.

What you are looking for is a gallery that has a manageable number of artists, and space large enough to show everyone's work, including yours.

In researching a gallery, there are two important areas of consideration. The first is financial and the second is developmental.

For the emerging artist developmental considerations are crucial in selecting galleries. By developmental, I mean how will they develop your career, and related to that, how will they present your art in their gallery. There are galleries who collect artists. That is, they are not discriminative in their selection of artists. Their motto is "the more the merrier." Usually, these are the galleries that demand the most stringent and restrictive agreements from their artists. They may claim to represent fifty or more artists. No gallery can represent fifty artists well. Unless the space is gargantuan, they are probably showing thirty artists with twenty artists having their works hidden in the storage room. This is not a good situation, and to make matters worse, their restrictive agreements prevent artists from pulling out of such galleries. What you are looking for is a gallery that has a manageable number of artists and a space large enough to show everyone's work including yours.

Another situation to exercise caution is the artist's gallery, that is, the gallery owned by an artist who shows his or her own work. It is just human nature that the best display spaces will be reserved for the owner, and they will sell their work with much greater enthusiasm than their other artists. On more than a few occasions I have known owner-artists to steer their other artists' collectors to their own work.

> *Every gallery will promise to sell your work, but not all galleries keep their promises. Just like artists, some galleries sell well and some do not.*

Next, you are looking for a gallery that devotes time, money and resources on developing their artists' careers. They should have a web site that shows every artist's work and is kept current. They also should have advertising presence in major art collector publications such as *Southwest Art, American Art Review, Art in America, Arts and Antiques*, etc. If they do not advertise in these publications, you can be pretty well assured that their artists will not receive editorial coverage on their pages. Every gallery will promise to sell your work, but not every gallery will work to develop your career or even promise to.

For the first-time gallery seeker, financial considerations

are not as important, but they still should be researched. Most galleries will promise to sell your work, but not all galleries keep their promises. Just like artists, some galleries sell well and some do not. Obviously, your chance of making sales are better in a gallery that actually makes sales. It is nice to be seen, but an occasional check is also nice. If the gallery is close to your home, you can attend shows and check the wall for "red dots." If attending the gallery's shows is not possible, you might contact a few of their artists to see if they will disclose some information on their sales.

Most galleries do pay their artists promptly, but there is a sizable minority who have reputations for "slow pay" or "no pay." These are the galleries to avoid — not only because of the money, but because of the psychological stress it puts on the artist's life

Even more frustrating for the artist are those galleries who sell, but never pay their artists on a timely basis. There are some galleries who won't pay unless the artist discovers a piece has been sold. It is hard enough to sell a painting, but when you do, you would like to get paid for it. Most galleries do pay their artists promptly, but there is a sizable minority who have reputations for being "slow pay" or even "no pay." These are galleries to avoid — not only because of the money situation, but because of the psychological stress that these galleries create for their artists.

There are no artist information bureaus providing information on how galleries treat their artists, but galleries quickly develop reputations, which you should investigate and consider. If a gallery is in another part of the country, there may be no reputation to go by. The best advice is to contact artists who already show in the gallery. Just because an artist shows there, it doesn't mean they're happy. Call or email them. Most will give you a true insight into the gallery's practices.

New galleries are the best candidates for new artists. They are actually seeking artists. Because they're new, the artists have little to go by except their own instincts. A majority of galleries don't survive two years, so there are sizable risks with showing with new galleries. Probably, the most important factor in evaluating new galleries is the amount of experience the owner or director has in the art field. An individual who has never managed a gallery is not a good bet to survive.

Whether it is a new gallery or established gallery, an artist without a gallery may have to take risks in order to show work. Also it is best to leave your ego in the studio. Artists sometimes will reject galleries because they feel their work is superior to the other art in the gallery. Once you get into your first gallery, then you can begin to be picky about subsequent galleries. Artists should not underestimate the importance of having at least one gallery showing their art.

Recruiting galleries depends on a simple objective: to get your artwork before the gallery individual who makes the decisions on new artists. There are three basic approaches to achieve this.

8. Three approaches

Recruiting galleries depends on a simple objective: getting your artwork before the individual who makes the decisions on new artists for the gallery. Most books on artist business outline a procedure for accomplishing this. I call this the *traditional approach*, and for gallery directors and owners who view themselves as traditionalists, this approach may be the right choice. But in this age of the internet, traditionalists are becoming a dying breed, and that approach has become less successful.

There is not a single strategy that applies to every situation. The artist's recruiting campaign depends on both the artist's situation and the disposition of the target galleries. A successful recruiting campaign considers both of these factors.

For instance, an artist who lives in a major city has a different situation than one who lives in a rural Midwest town. What economic and social resources does the artist possess? The artist's personality also comes into play. What may work for a naturally assertive extrovert will probably not work for a passive introvert.

How you approach a gallery in your own market is quite different than the way you need to approach a gallery in other markets. Also, for the artist without any gallery representation the process is different from one who already is represented by one or more galleries.

Regardless of the situation, there are some constants. First, research before you act. Before launching your campaign, you need to have as much information as possible. Second, you need to do an audit of your resources and networking possibilities. Lastly, you need to evaluate your own personality, and what activities you can do comfortably. Whenever you absolutely hate a process, you're going to do everything possible to avoid that task. If we want to evolve as artists and people, we must push beyond our comfort zone, but that process is much easier when we push gently.

Fundamentally, there are three tactical approaches an artist can adopt in recruiting galleries. The first is the traditional approach. The second is what I call the *alternative approach* which relies on some guerrilla tactics, and the third is a *promotional approach*. Each has its advantages and each has its disadvantages. The right approach is the one that works.

Traditional approach

The traditional approach is one which most galleries pay at least some lip service, but often that is all it is.

In the traditional method, the artist first approaches the gallery and inquires about their policy for selecting new artists. Most galleries have such policies, but they will often respond with the claim, "We currently are not seeking new artists."

Some galleries accept and review portfolios only during certain times of the year. In the galleries with which I have been associated that was in January, our slowest month. Portfolio submissions usually included about a dozen slides of recent work, a professional resumé and an artist's statement. A self-addressed, stamped envelope would have to accompany the portfolio.

For the artist, this involves a quite a bit of work and great deal of expense. The time and expense may be worth it if the galleries actually reviewed these portfolios. Some do review these portfolios, but often the portfolios are relegated to the back of file cabinets or the job is pushed off to an intern or a low-level employee who is instructed to return the portfolio with a note rejecting the work. The artist is fortunate just to have the portfolio returned if not reviewed.

There are many galleries, especially the major galleries, who still insist on following these guidelines. However, there has been a strong movement from hard copy and slides to digital components. For the artist, digital media is much cheaper than traditional media. Still, there is an issue of whether even these digital portfolios are ever reviewed.

You can't force the gallery directors to like and appreciate your work, but if you get your work before them, you've fulfilled your primary objective.

Some galleries require online submissions. For the artist, this almost assures that "somebody" will see the work, and with shrinking gallery staffs, it is a job that may fall to the gallery director. You can't force the gallery directors to like and appreciate your work, but if you get your work before them you've fulfilled your primary objective.

A substantial problem with the traditional approach is that you are asking for permission to show your work. If that permission is rejected ("I'm sorry, we're not currently seeking new artists.") or pushed off into the future ("We only review new artist in January."), the artist has no recourse, but to accept the rejection. In art as in life, if you don't want a "no," don't ask for permission.

Alternative approach

In the traditional approach, the goal is to arrange a formal review of your work with the gallery director or the person who selects new gallery artists. Besides the problem of immediate rejection, there is also the reality that gallery directors are reluctant to interview new artists. And it is also one of the reasons why gallery directors indicate they are not seeking new artists. What they are really not seeking is interviewing new artists. Who want to be placed in a situation where you have to deliver bad news?

A critique is a less stressful camouflage for a review. Asking for a critique is a way to stroke a gallery director's ego.

There is another consideration that comes into play here. When gallery directors come across art they like and think they can sell, they will take the initiative to pursue the artist. So fundamentally, the job of the artist is just to get their work before the gallery director (or the person who makes the decision on new artists) without the stress associated with formal reviews.

With this in mind, the artist is better off avoiding formal interviews. So instead of trying to arrange a formal review of the work, the artist attempts to secure an informal review. In art parlance, we call this a *critique*. A critique is a less stressful camouflage for a review. It is less stressful for both the artist and the gallery director, because no decisions are requested and none have to be made.

Asking for a critique is a way to stroke a gallery director's ego. I know many gallery directors who even enjoy giving critiques. It is a testament that they are experts on what makes art good and saleable. We cannot overlook the obvious psychology that's involved here. If an artist has established a friendly rapport with a gallery director, there is a very good chance he or she will agree to critique the artist's work. This is what friendly people do for each other.

Getting a critique by a local gallery director is much simpler to achieve than an out-of-market gallery. The process for the local gallery is more informal and relies heavily on your interpersonal skills. Whereas, the process for out-of-market galleries requires more planning and relies less on your interpersonal skills and more on your marketing skills. However, both situations require the requisites that were discussed in Chapter 3.

Local gallery

For most artists, their first gallery is a local gallery. So we may also view this situation for recruiting your first gallery. Again, the goal is simply to get your art in front of the gallery director. Of course, you may prefer a formal review, but an informal critique may be just as effective, and a lot less stressful.

As an artist, you probably have a fairly good knowledge of the galleries in your area as well as the people who manage them. If you don't, then your first task is to do this research. Once you have narrowed down your choice of galleries, then you want to establish your presence in the gallery as a welcome visitor. This means attending shows and other events that the gallery may produce. The most welcome visitor is one who actually buys art, but in today's art environment, galleries are appreciative when anyone shows up for their events.

In order to attend these events, you need to know when they are scheduled. Signing a gallery's visitor book will get you on the gallery's mailing list. Include both your mailing address and your email address. Many galleries communicate with their collectors exclusively through email. In addition, you should visit their website and their Facebook page. Many galleries offer eletters to their web visitors. So sign up for those as well. Similarly, when you visit their Facebook page, they may offer sign-ups as well, and give the gallery a "like."

Obviously, creating presence in a gallery requires time, and it is not something you can achieve in a few days or even weeks. You know you have "arrived" when the gallery director greets you by name, and may even recognize you as an artist. There is one bit of caution here. *Presence* does not mean *pest*. Showing up every week at the gallery to talk art will quickly wear out your welcome.

At some point in your relationship with the gallery director, you are ready to ask the question. You approach this as an appreciative favor.

Here is a typical request:

"I love your gallery and the kind of art you show. I really respect your taste in art and it would be a great favor if you might critique mine. I am not exactly certain what direction I need to go, and it would be certainly helpful to get an opinion I trust."

How could any gallery director refuse? Of course they can, but you have a much better chance than saying, "I would like you to review my art to be considered for your gallery." Again, the goal is simply to get the art in front of the gallery director.

You might also add that you understand that this may be an imposition, and you would certainly do it at the most convenient time for the director.

Your critique

I have been asked and have given many art critiques. I tell artists that I am not a painter, but I know the pictorial qualities that appeal to collectors. So when I do a critique, I concentrate on those qualities. Even given this proviso, I have had some uncomfortable moments in these critiques. These occur with artists who are not seeking critical suggestion, but unequivocal praise.

Even though I am one of those people who strive to say something positive before I would make a negative comment, I still have encountered artists who have become antagonistic during the critique. When this happens, I abbreviate the critique with a few positive comments, and make the mental note that I never want to represent this artist.

There are some gallery directors who believe that a critique should be all critical because they feel that artists can only learn from their mistakes. So when you ask for a critique be prepared for a criticism. Even if you feel the criticism is unwarranted, try to accept it without rancor, and resist the temptation to defend the work. You might ask suggestions on how you might have painted it differently, but avoid challenging the critique-giver. I have heard from more than a few artists who felt originally that the critique was unfair, and then later realized the criticism was justified.

Some gallery directors believe that a critique should be all critical. So when you ask for a critique be prepared to be criticized.

At the end of the critique express your appreciation for the director's time, even if you didn't appreciate the critique. If the critique was particularly harsh, there is probably little chance in getting into that gallery then or in the future. In most cases, the critique will be mixed with both positive and negative comments, and you should give some consideration to both.

As I've noted often, if the gallery director is impressed with the work and believes s/he can sell it, there is a good chance of receiving a gallery invitation. And even if an invitation is not forthcoming, it does not mean the director did not appreciate the art. On many occasions I have told artists that I thought they were close to mastering their work, and that I would be interested in seeing subsequent work. On a few occasions, I have even added a few of these artists to my gallery when their work became a bit more accomplished. So the point is, whatever the outcome of the critique, don't burn your bridges with a defensive attitude.

Other opportunities

Critiques are just one way to get your work before the gallery director. Others are direct and some may be a bit circuitous, but artists must use every device they can if they want to succeed.

Most galleries will host their own juried shows or host shows for other organizations. Although I am somewhat dubious of the benefits of these shows, if the show is at one of your target galleries, then it does provide an opportunity to get your work before the gallery director. As an owner and a gallery director, nothing captures your attention as much as red dots. So selling work under any circumstance may attract gallery attention.

Art organizations will often negotiate with galleries to host their shows. For instance, the local plein air group in Colorado produces a show every year in one of the local galleries. Even for the artist who does not normally join some groups, it is usually worth the moderate expense to join these groups, especially if they are active in show production. There is little down side in participating in these shows, and you may even sell a painting.

Philanthropic organizations also hold auctions at local galleries. In most cases, the charity is seeking a full donation. In some of the major auctions, the artist may receive payment that is even greater than they would have gotten from their own galleries. Artists have approached me about the advisability of participating in these shows. If the show pays the artist gallery rates, then there is nothing to lose, and you do gain some visibility and perhaps even a sale. In the cases where the artist receives no compensation, and the art can sell for any price, these

> *Gallery directors are often recruited to jury shows. This is an excellent way to get your work before a targeted gallery director.*

shows are not a great choice unless you have a strong affinity for the charity. However, if the auction is in a target gallery, it may be worth the donation to get the attention of the gallery director.

If your target gallery offers framing, it is an easy matter to get your painting before the gallery director. In today's challenging economic environment for galleries, the gallery director may also be involved in frame sales. And even in cases, where the framing is managed by another individual, you can always ask the gallery director their opinion. "Should I get a gold or black frame?"

Although major galleries, who frame, may not be influenced by an artist's framing business, it may be a factor for a secondary gallery. And of course, there are galleries who insist in framing all of the art in their gallery. This is an issue that will be discussed later in the book.

I have had many artists stop by my gallery on the way to their framer just to get my opinion. I am certain there was no other ulterior motive for asking my opinion. These visits never bothered me if they were infrequent and I liked the artist.

Gallery directors are often recruited to jury shows. This is also another excellent way to get your work before the gallery director. This provides you some additional insight into the gallery director's preferences. If a gallery director doesn't select your piece for a show, it is a reasonable expectation that you will have little success in getting into his or her gallery. If they do select your work, it does not guarantee they will be interested in representing your work, but, at least, it's an optimistic sign.

The out-of-market gallery

In considering an out-of-market gallery, the most promising market will be an art destination market. These are markets that attract high level of tourists, and a key attraction for these tourists is the art. Santa Fe, Taos, Laguna Beach, Sedona, Hilton Head are all markets that fit this description. The obvious reason for looking at these markets is that more galleries mean more gallery slots for artists. Plus, the local artist community probably does not have enough talented artists to fill these slots. In large city galleries, the community of artists competing for limited gallery slots is large, and the competition for these slots is intense. In these cities, gallery directors often prefer to work with local artists as opposed to out-of-market artists.

The process of securing a local or home gallery relies heavily on the artist's interpersonal skill whereas for out-of-market galleries the focus is on the art and the reputation of the artist. Nevertheless, the objective is the same: getting your work in front of the directors of your target galleries. The plan for recruiting out-of-market galleries is more structured. The difficulty in these situations deals with the problems of proximity. Unlike the local gallery, it is much more difficult to establish a friendly relationship with the gallery director. Without the opportunity to exploit this relationship, you are going to depend more on your art and less on your sparkling personality. Even so, personality factors still come into play.

The process of securing a local or home gallery stresses the interpersonal activity whereas for the out-of-market galleries, the focus is on the art, and the reputation of the artist.

Step 1: Research

The first step is to determine where you hope to recruit a gallery. How an artist paints and the subject matter influence the artist's potential in different art markets. Art that would be appreciated in Nantucket might not have the same reception in Taos. For example, watercolor is much more esteemed in the East than it is in the West. Cowboy themes sell in the West whereas marine art rarely does. Of course, major art destinations will present a diversity of galleries serving a diversity of tastes, but each locale still has its own artistic tendencies. For instance, Santa Fe has many galleries that feature contemporary abstracts, but history and proximity favor art that is identified as "Southwestern." Artists who paint in a Southwestern style will have a much better chance to recruit a gallery in Santa Fe than they will in Maui.

While much of your research can be done on the internet, eventually you will want to visit the gallery in person. From the internet, you can get a general feel about a gallery's art and artists, but you can only gain insight into a gallery's human energy by actual observation.

Step 2: Visit prospective galleries

When you visit a new art market, you have three primary goals. First, you want to determine which galleries are the best prospects for your art. Second, you want to investigate the human energies of these prospective galleries to determine how comfortable you would fit interpersonally in these galleries. And thirdly, you want to ascertain who are the decision-makers in the gallery, and hopefully make a positive contact with these individuals.

Besides the basic research, the artist should come equipped with necessary accoutrements for the trip. The most important of these is your business card and your mini-portfolio. You should also take a few of your original paintings — they do not have to be framed but they should be some of your best work. This may seem a bit presumptuous, but unexpected circumstances often arise when it would be beneficial to have actual work to show.

More practical items would include a small notebook and pen to make notes on the spot. Although we may often assume that we will remember what we have seen, a trip to an art destination can become overwhelming. Because of this, I always suggest visiting your best gallery prospects first while your mind is still fresh and not deluged by the art.

When you enter in each of your prospective targets, you must keep in mind your three-fold purpose of your gallery investigation: appropriateness of your art, the human energy, and the name of the decision-maker and their title. At the very least, you will want to get the gallery director's business card. And consider it a real bonus if you have an opportunity to meet the director.

After leaving the gallery, but before visiting the next one, you should take some time to record your thoughts in your notebook. Again, it is easy to think you will remember everything but impressions of galleries can begin to converge. And if you had an opportunity to speak to the gallery director, make a note of what you spoke about. This will be important when you follow-up this visit.

After you have visited the prime gallery candidates, you are free to explore other possibilities. However, a second visit to your best gallery prospects would be advisable. The second visit is to confirm your initial impressions, and perhaps, a second opportunity to talk to the gallery director, especially if you did not have a chance during the first visit.

In your conversations with gallery staff, you neither have to conceal nor proclaim yourself as an artist. If the subject arises, don't prevaricate. If you don't think of yourself as an artist then how will others view you? That admission might result in a quick end of the conversation, or it might also result in the response, "What kind of art do you do?" Then you have an opportunity to brandish your mini-portfolio.

Hopefully, your art junket resulted in identifying a few potential galleries for follow-up when you return home.

Step 3: The follow-up

It is important to follow-up immediately upon returning home. First, your own impressions of galleries will quickly fade, and any impression you have made during your visit will fade even quicker.

The follow-up contact utilizes the personal greeting card in Chapter 3 on requisites. The card should be addressed by hand to the gallery director. If you actually spoke with the gallery director, the card should express your appreciation for the conversation, and make some note to the content of the conversation. Whether you spoke to the director or not, you should mention how the gallery was one of your favorite galleries from your trip, and, that the gallery would be one you would aspire to show your art. The note might be concluded with notation of your website on the back of the card.

If the gallery director remembers you favorably and he or she is attracted to the image on the card, there is a good chance the director may visit your website. And again, all you hope to do is to get your work before the gallery director. If there is interest, you may receive a call.

If the card has not evoked a response, then you might send a second card with a CD of your work. If the gallery has explicit information on their website regarding new artist submissions, you should follow their guidelines, but again make reference to your visit in your cover letter.

If none of these efforts result in a gallery response, you can surmise that for whatever reason they are not interested in carrying your work. Despite this, you should maintain some permanent record of the gallery and its director. When you plan to visit the same gallery in the future, you might send off another greeting card to the gallery director indicating how much you are looking forward to visiting their gallery.

This alternative approach should not be just directed to a

single gallery, but to several prospects. Again, all you need is get your work before the right person and you may receive that welcoming phone call or email.

The promotional approach

It is the rare artist that enjoys recruiting galleries to represent them. A third approach is to have galleries recruit you. Some artists have been successful in using advertising and other promotional efforts to attract galleries. Like all of the approaches that have been discussed, there are no guarantees that promotional efforts will be successful. The advantage of promotion is that if you are successful, galleries will come to you. The disadvantage is that promotion costs money, and few artists have the resources to promote effectively.

A promotional plan that involves frequent advertising will be expensive.The artist may consider a one-time investment in advertising. For this to be really cost-effective, the advertising should be employed in conjunction with a show. If the artist already has a gallery affiliation, the show may be with this gallery. If the artist is not affiliated with a gallery, there is the possibility of renting a gallery space for a few weeks. The gallery owner may be motivated to reduce the rent or even forego it if there is a promise of a full-page advertisement. After all, the advertising would benefit the gallery as well.

A full-page ad is major expense in all of the national art periodicals, but if the promotion is going to succeed, it has to include a full page in one of these publications. A second alternative that would be less costly (and less effective) is to join with one or two other artists and split the costs. This alternative can open all kinds of other problems that accompany any cooperative venture. If the artist fails to sell a painting or recruit a gallery, it can be very demoralizing if the other artists sell and receive gallery invitations

Because of the high costs involved, I have suggested to artists that they need to allow sufficient time before committing to such an advertised show. First, you need sufficient time to create a body of compelling paintings, and you'll want to hold the show during a strong art sales month. You are going to have a much better response in November than you will in January or July.

There are other less costly promotional alternatives that reach galleries. Unfortunately, most rarely deliver what they promise, and the artist would be wise to investigate these closely. A promoter of such events and programs should be able to supply you a list of artists who have had success with them.

I cover advertising in greater detail in the next chapter, "Does advertising work?"

9. Does advertising work?

I have noted that new artists find their way into galleries, even in cases when the galleries had stated they were not interested in any new artists. The primary explanation is that the gallery director saw the artist's work; liked it, and then recruited the artist. In many cases, the artist's work may have been seen in a magazine. From there, the gallery director probably visited the artist's website where he or she was contacted. So, indeed advertising can be effective tool in gallery recruitment.

In our gallery, we recruited about a quarter of our new artists after seeing their work in magazines. This included both editorial and advertising features. Although magazine media is on the decline, gallery directors still read art magazines, if for nothing else, to see their own ads.

In my workshop, *The Artist in Search of Gallery*, I cite three examples of artist's use of advertising.

In the first case, a middle-aged female artist wanted to kick-start her art career. She and her husband had the resources to buy six months of full-page ads in a major arts magazine. The investment at the time was about $15,000. Every ad featured a single painting, which sold for more than the cost of the ad.

At the end of the six months, she sold every painting that was featured plus several additional paintings. Four major galleries also recruited her. She believes that advertising developed her career five years faster than if she had not advertised.

In the second case, three young emerging artists, who painted together decided to split a single page ad in another major art publication. The cost for each was just over $1000, and each featured a painting that was above $1,000. They, too, were successful in that each sold their painting, and each received at least one offer of gallery representation.

The last case was a middle-aged male artist who had painted professionally for over ten years. He was currently represented by a minor gallery, which had no budget to advertise. His sales were marginal, and showing no signs of improvement. He was good, but not an exceptional landscape painter. With great difficulty, he scraped together enough money to buy a half-page ad in a regional publication whose editorial focus was appropriate for his art.

Although the publication had a fairly large readership, his ad failed to generate one response from either collector or gallery. For him, it was a devastating experience both financially and psychologically.

If you cannot afford financially and emotionally a zero response from your ad, then don't take the risk.

Artists often overlook the psychological risks that are involved in advertising. When you place your work before 100,000 readers, and not a single reader feels the work is compelling enough to respond, it certainly will deflate anyone's confidence. This, indeed, affected this landscape artist. After that experience, he quit painting for several years. Although I should note that despite this experience, he eventually returned to painting and has come to enjoy some success.

There are lessons to be learned from these examples. If you

cannot afford financially and emotionally a zero response from your ad, then don't take the risk.

In terms of the advertisement itself, select a piece that is one of your strongest and most representative work. Choose a magazine whose editorial focus directly relates to your subject matter and style. If you can't afford a full page, you are better off sharing a page with other artists or attempt to find a gallery that will be willing to share costs. Ads that are smaller than a full page always look small and lack punch.

Many exhibitions arrange with art magazines to offer their artists a major discount for supportive exhibition advertising. Usually, the ads are a quarter page for a rate that may be half the magazine's normal rate. I have received mixed reaction to these ads. I have known artists who sold the piece and attracted the attention of a gallery, and I have known others who achieved neither. On balance, if the artist can comfortably afford the expense of the ad and is willing to rationalize the expenditure purely on "exposure" principles, then I say go for it. But the principle still applies, never spend money for advertising when you feel you must sell the painting to justify the expenditure.

With the emergence of the internet, online advertising opportunities for artists have dramatically risen. Some of these programs may be worth the effort to investigate, but few of these programs generate a response to justify the expense and time to participate in these programs.

Generally, the only media that deserve the artist's attention are the national and regional art magazines. Choose the magazine that features the kind of art that you produce. Several of these publications include additional editorial coverage, which can be particularly valuable if you are doing a show. The rates on rate cards are not inflexible, and sometimes for first-time advertisers discounts can be negotiated. Collectors are rarely hesitant to request discounts from galleries and artists, so why should the artist be hesitant to ask for discounts from media? All they can say is "no."

Art advertising differs from other products in that repetition is not necessary. If a collector appreciates the work, he or she will act without needing to see multiple exposures to the art. However, every new collector will usually want to see more of the work before making a significant investment in a piece of art. This is one of the reasons why a supporting website is necessary for every artist.

Because repetition is not required in art advertising, you only need to place one ad to determine if the particular magazine is right for your art. If an ad fails to generate response the first time, there is little likelihood that subsequent advertising is going to be any more successful, regardless of what the advertising salesperson says. Because of this, it is never advisable to sign a contract for multiple insertions.

Does advertising work? The jury is still out, but there is one piece of advice that applies: never advertise if you cannot afford the financial and psychological trauma of failed advertising.

10. The formal interview

Once you have secured an interview, the next step is to prepare for the formal presentation to the gallery. For this you will need both a portfolio and several paintings. A fundamental question is whether you should show the gallery a diversity of work or to focus on those paintings that you believe the gallery would most likely respond positively.

Generally you should show your strongest work in both your portfolio and in the paintings that you choose to bring. However, the work should be consistent with the images that were used in securing the interview. Common sense also applies. If the gallery is very traditional, leave your modern, conceptual paintings at home.

An artist may paint in several different styles, especially when the artist also works in different media. This provides a dilemma for the gallery, because collectors must be educated on the specific character of the artist's work. If there is no specific character, then it is difficult to effectively promote the artist. In order for an artist to ultimately develop a collector following, the work must have a distinctive "look." This look is in both in technical style as well as subject matter. I know some painters worry about being trapped by this look, but for all artists, developing a distinctive style of painting is crucial.

One of the preconditions that artists must consider before seeking gallery representation is whether they have found such a style and range of subject matter that can be consistently presented.

At my former gallery, we represented a nationally renowned realist. Although he painted different subject matters from interiors to landscapes to still lifes and even figurative work, he still retained that definable technical quality, and even with such diverse subject matter, all of the paintings retained an identifiable, distinctive quality. A few years ago, he moved to West Coast for a year, and for his own enjoyment and experimentation he painted some impressionistic seascapes. The paintings were very striking, and we discovered that they were as appealing to collectors as his realist paintings. These paintings sold for the same price as his realist paintings, but they took much less time to paint. Despite the acceptance of collectors for the work, he recognized the necessity of retaining his distinctive realism, and discontinued offering the impressionistic work.

To the formal interview bring your strongest pieces even if you have to borrow a few from collectors or other galleries. The pieces should be consistent with the work that attracted the gallery in the first place.

Paintings always present themselves better with frames, but for presentation purposes, everything does not have to be framed. Those that you do bring to show should be framed well. When you move into galleries, frames must be gallery quality. That does not mean they have to be museum quality, but the gallery must not have any reservations about displaying the work. As a general rule, gold frames are always acceptable followed by black frames. There are a few galleries that only accept gold frames. Avoid excessive ornamentation, and unusual materials or colors. If you're painting oils, try to keep away from linen mats unless the paintings are very small. For your gallery presentation, choose frames that you plan to use in the gallery. Nice ready-mades are acceptable in most cases.

With most galleries, framing is the responsibility of the artist. Since the paintings are on consignment, they should be framed by the artist and not the gallery. Galleries have often tempted artists with the promise to frame the paintings for them. Of course this can be financially attractive and can reduce expenses for the artist. However problems can arise when the artist needs to move the painting out of the gallery. I know artists who have had to leave paintings in galleries from which they had withdrawn because they could not afford to pay the gallery the cost of the frames. Nevertheless, because framing is such a major investment for artists, sometimes artists are forced to allow the gallery to frame their work.

Some artists also try to develop signature frames, which they will either design themselves or work with a framer to originate a framing style expressly for their work. This can be an appealing option for artists, but unless they have the skills to make their own frames it can be an expensive alternative.

Although many artists are understandably anxious about these formal presentations, they are usually amiable situations. Some gallery directors will offer specific criticisms, while others will not. Criticism is not always a negative omen for the artist. If the gallery director takes time to offer insightful suggestions, it usually means he or she is serious about the work.

Even if you do not think some criticism is fair or accurate, don't become defensive or apologetic. One of the goals of an art director should be to help you become a better artist. If you become defensive or angry, then the gallery director will have real reservations about bringing you into the gallery.

Finally and very important: the relationship between a gallery and the artist is beyond business — it is a personal relationship. Regardless of how great the art is, no gallery wants to be associated with a moody, temperamental and unfriendly artist. So regardless of how the presentation is progressing try to keep a smile on your face and be gracious for the opportunity to show your work.

In addition to presenting actual paintings, most galleries will like to view the artist's portfolio. Even when most of that information and visuals are presented on the artist's website, many gallery directors would also want to see hard copies of the artist's bio, resumé or curriculum vitae, an artist's statement and perhaps images of additional work. The gallery will need this information for their own staff, but also for information that must be developed for collectors. When a collector requests information on the artist, the gallery will want to have collateral materials to give to their collectors. It is not professional for gallery staff to tell collectors they should go to the artist's website to learn more about the artist.

Even if you do not think some criticism is fair or accurate, don't become defensive or apologetic for the paintings. Gallery directors do not want to deal with artists who cannot accept criticism and positive suggestion. Losing your composure never helps your cause.

In many cases, the formal interview will conclude with a decision, especially if that decision is a positive one. The gallery director may even request that the artist leave some of the work from the interview. The gallery director might also indicate they will contact the artist when they have a decision. This is not a clear omen of rejection, for gallery directors often want to get staff input on new artists, and in many galleries, the gallery owner has to approve each new artist.

You should conclude the interview with an appreciation for the opportunity to interview. In addition, you should also express your pleasure to be considered by the gallery. Gallery directors want to know if their artists are excited about joining their gallery. Even if you are asked whether you have any questions, it is better to postpone discussions on commissions, prices, etc., until a formal invitation has been extended.

For the emerging artist, there are only a few items that are open to negotiation with a new gallery, but these items can be very important, especially if the gallery relationship is to succeed.

11. Negotiation and agreements

When an artist joins a new gallery it probably has its own gallery-artist agreement, and expects new artists to abide by its content. Most of these agreements have provisions that are fairly standard and most of these are rarely negotiated. However, several items in these agreements should be examined and perhaps negotiated before signing.

Most artists are reluctant to question these provisions because they do not want to antagonize the gallery. This reluctance is well founded, for indeed, most galleries will have second thoughts about an artist who challenges every provision in their artist agreement. Artists who attempt to put forth their own gallery-artist agreement will probably be shown the door.

The gallery-artist agreement describes the basis by which the gallery and the artist will do business. In some regards, the agreement is only a piece of paper, and only as good as the integrity of the signers. Those aspects of the agreement that outline the fundamental business activity of the gallery should not be challenged. For instance, if the agreement stipulates the artist will receive payment for all sales during the month by the fifteenth day of the following month, then this is how the gallery handles payments and how they pay all of their artists. A new artist should not expect to be treated any differently.

Commissions and discounts

Most galleries have a standard commission for new artists. In most cases that gallery commission is 50%. If the artist is well established and has a prestigious reputation, the commission rate can be negotiated lower. Some of these artists may only be subject to a 30% commission and in some rare cases even lower. Unless you are one of these artists, you cannot expect to negotiate a rate any lower than 50%.

Most of these agreements stipulate that the gallery will not discount any work unless approved by the artist. In reality, even with that provision in the agreement, galleries will always discount work with or without the approval of the artist. All savvy collectors expect discounts. And in the heat of a negotiation, the discount may be necessary to close a sale. I included a reasonable discount provision in my artist agreement, I could discount up to ten percent without contacting the artist. If I discounted more than that, I either contacted the artist or took the discount out of my commission.

> ***Unless the artist contributes significantly to a gallery's sales, galleries are not motivated to respond to the artist's concerns. If the artist complains, the gallery can always replace the artist with one that won't.***

The point is that even if the provision is in the agreement, there are going to be discounts without the artist's approval. If the discount appears reasonable, most artists will not challenge it. However, excessive discounts without the artist's approval should make the artist re-evaluate his or her relationship with the gallery.

Unless the artist contributes significantly to a gallery's sales, galleries are not particularly motivated to respond to the artist's concerns regarding their discount policy. If the artist complains, they can always replace the artist with one who won't. Now this is not to say all galleries act in this matter, but it is certainly not uncommon.

Most agreements include the provision that a painting will not leave the gallery without the approval of the artist. This also contradicts the reality of gallery operations. Most galleries allow collectors to take a piece of art home for their "approval." This is especially true for a gallery's best collectors. A gallery might request a credit card number for security, but some may not even seek this protection.

The gallery business is built on trust. Not only does the collector have to trust the gallery, but the gallery has to trust the collector. Selling art on approval is one example of this trust. Now, does this mean a gallery is going to allow a complete stranger to walk out of the gallery with a $10,000 piece of art? No, but it is a necessary sales tool in dealing with collectors.

Now consider the situation where the gallery contacted an artist to see if a collector could take the painting home on approval. If the artist rejected the gallery's request, it would seriously jeopardize the gallery's relationship with the collector, and also the collector's intention to purchase the art.

Now if the collector does abscond with the art, it is the obligation of the gallery to pay the artist for the "sale." I should note in twenty years of selling art, with hundreds of pieces being sold on approval, I have never had a painting or sculpture that was not either sold or returned to the gallery.

Standard provisions

Other provisions are fairly standard as well. The artist is responsible for the shipping to the gallery, while the gallery is responsible for shipping to the artist. In rare occasions, the artist is responsible for both, but this is usually in the case of specific shows, which usually have their own exhibition agreement.

The gallery is responsible for the safeguarding of the work while in its custody. The agreement will stipulate the gallery maintains adequate insurance. All galleries tell their artists they have this insurance, but for struggling galleries this is one expense that is often slashed. I have never had an artist request to see my insurance policy, and even if one were to be produced there are no guarantees that it is current.

Galleries are also responsible for protecting the artist's frames. Nothing is more irksome to an artist than to have paintings returned with damaged frames. Although some artists will contact their galleries for compensation, most don't. In defense of galleries, it is difficult to totally avoid some frame damage. Galleries are continually moving frames and even when they attempt to be careful, dings can occur. In the galleries that I have been associated we would repair frames that were damaged, but not all galleries will do this readily.

Agreements also give the artist the right to inspect the gallery books in regard to inventory and sales. I have never known an artist to make this request, except when they were leaving a gallery and they wanted the names and addresses of all those who have purchased their work. Most galleries will refuse this request if they know the artist is leaving the gallery. The gallery knows the artist will provide this information to their new gallery, and they will be adamant in their refusal. Galleries guard their collector list with great scrupulousness. Some galleries are reluctant to share with the artist sales information about the collector even at the time of sale. Although this right is usually included in the gallery-artist agreement, most galleries will not abide by it. Of course legal action is possible, but few artists take this route.

Region of exclusivity

There are provisions in the gallery-artist agreements that do warrant attention, and perhaps negotiation. The new gallery will have the exclusive right to represent and sell the artist's work in a designated region. The gallery will seek the largest region possible. Some galleries may even seek national exclusivity, but the exclusive area is usually limited. The area may be defined as "within 100 miles of Atlanta, Georgia" or for the "state of Texas."

The right of exclusion can become troubling when the gallery is located near the artist's studio. Since the artist is excluded from selling art within this area, the artist is prohibited from making sales out of their own studio.

The artist loses more control as the area of exclusivity increases. For instance, a Taos gallery might demand to be the artist's exclusive gallery in New Mexico. This exclusivity will prevent the artist from seeking a gallery in Santa Fe, despite the fact that these markets are much different in the number and type of collector they attract.

Galleries believe they have this right to this exclusion because they have devoted resources and time to develop an artist's career, and they don't want to share the benefits of their effort with other galleries.

This area of exclusion is subject to negotiation and most

galleries will have some flexibility in this designation.

This right of exclusion can become troubling when the gallery is located near the artist's studio. Since the artist is excluded from selling any art within this area, the artist is prevented from making sales out of the studio. When the artist has developed a local collector base, he may negotiate the right to sell out of the studio, and compensate the gallery with some commission for those sales. Some galleries seek full commissions, but the percentage is often less than a full commission. However, if the sale is made to one of the gallery's collectors, the artist is obligated to give the gallery a full commission. This is a real test for the artist's integrity and often puts the artist in an ethical conundrum when sales are made to an individual who is both a collector of the gallery and the artist.

The gallery-artist agreement may prevent an artist from donating to charitable exhibitions. This may not be totally a problem because artists are constantly badgered to donate art to local charity auctions.

Then, there is a matter of the artist participating in exhibitions in his or her local area. If the exhibition is held in another gallery, the artist may be prohibited from participating or be obligated to pay a commission to both galleries. I once hosted an exhibition of local plein air painters, and the agreement called for the gallery to receive a 25% commission. One of the artists who was represented by a local gallery sold a piece in the show. Because his gallery agreement called for a 50% commission on art that was sold locally, he was forced to pay both galleries, leaving only 25% for himself.

The agreement may even prevent the artist from donating a painting to charitable exhibitions. This may not be totally a problem because artists are constantly badgered to donate art for local charity auctions.

Allowing an artist to participate in a prestigious exhibition may benefit the gallery, but many galleries do not share this view.

Term and termination of agreement

The next point that may be negotiated in the gallery-artist agreement is the term of the agreement. Most agreements call for a term of one year. I believe this initial term should be shorter. In the majority of cases, an artist will know whether a gallery will generate sales in the first three months. If a gallery does not sell a single piece of art in the first three months, it is a high probability that the gallery

The term of the initial agreement is inconsequential if there is a short notice period to terminate the agreement. Therefore for the artist, the termination provision in the agreement is more important than the term provision.

will never perform for the artist. So what is the point of keeping inventory tied up for a year in non-performing gallery?

In my own galleries, I suggested to new artists that the agreement should stipulate a trial period of three months, and at the end of the three months we both could evaluate our success or lack there of with both parties having the option to pull out of the arrangement without any hard feelings.

Related to the term of the agreement are the provisions for termination of the agreement. Most of these agreements allow either party to terminate the agreement with written notice. Some agreements call for a ninety-day notice, but some are as short as thirty days. So the term of the initial agreement is inconsequential if there is a short notice termination provision in the agreement. Therefore, for the artist, the termination provision in the agreement is more significant than the term provision.

Framing galleries

A few galleries require the artist to allow the gallery to frame all of the work that is to be shown in the gallery. On the surface, this benefits the artist since framing is a major expense. The primary concern for the artist is the attributed cost of the framing. Some agreements provide that the framing cost will be at a wholesale amount. But that amount may be somewhat arbitrary, and the cost of the painting will reflect on the retail cost of the art. The gallery, after all, wants to make a profit on their framing. The gallery framing charges may push up the cost of the piece to a point that curtails sales.

And then there are the issues when an artist wishes to withdraw work from the gallery. This can become a real problem when an artist wishes to completely leave a gallery. We encountered that exact problem with a new artist who joined our gallery. His previous gallery would not release the paintings until his accumulated framing bill was settled. It amounted to a few thousand dollars, and we ultimately had to advance the artist the money to retrieve his work.

The consignment agreement

Artist pricing is not specifically defined in the gallery-artist agreement except to note that the gallery is required to honor the prices on the consignment agreement. The consignment agreement may be a separate form or an addendum to the gallery-artist agreement. However, future consignments will (should) be recorded on a separate consignment sheet. The sheet indicates the physical specifications of the piece, the retail price and the gallery commission. The consignment agreement may also include provisions of sale regarding discounts, payments, etc. As I've noted, most galleries don't abide by these conditions.

Artists should design and produce their own consignment sheets, but without the provisions of sale verbiage. This saves the gallery the time and effort of recording the information, which they should appreciate. When a gallery insists on their own consignment sheets, problems always arise, because frequently the galleries will defer creating a sheet immediately because they are "just too busy."

> *Artists should design and produce their own consignment sheets. When galleries insist on using their own sheets, problems often arise when the gallery is "just too busy" to provide the sheet when work is dropped off at the gallery.*

Once the pieces are placed into inventory, no consignment sheet may ever be forthcoming. This is bad business practice for both the artist and the gallery, and could eventually lead to disputes.

Pricing

Most artists are uncertain what prices to ask for their work, especially prices in their first gallery. I have been asked several times who sets art prices — the gallery or the artist? My response is neither. Ultimately prices are set by the collectors, who by their purchases determine what the artist's price will be.

Pricing can become an ego-issue. We attribute value to the art according to its price. So an artist may say, "I'm as good as that artist, so I should get the same price for my work." Again, it does not work that way. The price is what the collectors will pay.

Although it is difficult to do, the artist should try to get away from this mindset that price determines the value of the painting. The value of the painting should be in the joy in creating the work, and ultimately the joy that the collector has in viewing and owning the painting.

You should normally rely on the gallery's judgement when setting prices — even if the price is less than you would like to realize. Galleries know their collectors and what they will pay for the gallery's work.

Often artists will have a distorted view of pricing because they sell a few paintings a year at fairly high prices. The question is not the highest prices you can sell a few paintings a year, but what price structure will allow you to sell several paintings a month.

I have often heard an artist say, "I need to get this amount out of a painting." Because you can sell paintings out of your studio for $500, it does not mean that a gallery can sell the same painting for $1000. In most cases, what you can sell the painting for is what the gallery can sell the painting for. The hope is that they can sell more paintings than you could alone.

The artist should normally rely on the gallery's judgment when setting prices — even if the price is less than you would like to realize. Galleries know their collectors, and what they will pay for work. What this price is depends on the gallery. An emerging art gallery cannot sell the art as the same price as a prestigious gallery whereas the coffee shop gallery cannot sell it at the same price as the emerging art gallery.

Because the gallery has certain price expectations regarding an artist's work, it will diminish their enthusiasm to sell work if they believe it is overpriced.

For this reason, an artist always hopes to land in a prestigious gallery with upscale collectors, because their prices will be higher. But the reason that prestigious galleries are prestigious is because they exhibit artists who have already achieved a reputation.

When the gallery has certain price expectations regarding an artist's work, it will diminish their enthusiasm to sell work if they believe it is overpriced. Galleries will often reluctantly accept the artist's prices even when they doubt their collectors will pay these prices. This uncertainty can be self-fulfilling.

New artist sales generate enthusiasm for the artist. In the next chapter, I discuss the importance of the first three months in a new gallery. Just as sales generate enthusiasm for the artist, the opposite is also the case. When sales are weak or nonexistent, the enthusiasm for the artist wanes very quickly. An artist does not want to risk sales with prices that are viewed as too high.

Finally, there is also the issue of price flexibility. It is much easier to raise your prices than to lower them. If your paintings go flying off the wall at your new gallery, then maybe they are priced too low. But you still have the option to raise them.

Almost in every situation, when in doubt about pricing, an artist is usually better off choosing the lower, rather than the higher prices for their work, especially in a new gallery.

The exhibition agreement

Exhibition agreements are common with prestigious shows, but when an artist does a show with their own gallery, there is often no written agreement. There should be. The exhibition agreement has elements of the gallery-artist agreement and of a consignment form. The exhibition agreement defines how revenues and costs will be allocated for an exhibition. Like the consignment agreement, it stipulates which paintings will be provided by the artist and the retail price of these paintings. The commission that the gallery or exhibition will receive is also included.

The artist needs to know what the total costs will be for each of the exhibition expenses. You don't want to pay half of the harpist's $500 fee for the opening party.

A major difference between the gallery agreement and the exhibition agreement regards shipping. In an exhibition agreement, the artist may be responsible for shipping to and from the gallery. In many cases, the show pieces remain with the gallery, but if they are shipped back, the artist may have to bear the cost.

The exhibition agreement also includes the provisions regarding attribution of expenses for exhibition expenses. This includes advertising, invitations and show opening expenses. In simple terms, the agreement states who pays for what. In some cases, these expenses are evenly split between the artist and the gallery. In some cases, the gallery assumes all of the expenses. When it comes to exhibition agreements, there is no standard agreement.

These provisions will impact the financial success of the show for the artist. Most galleries have their own policy regarding show expenses, and there are few items that are open for negotiation. However, just as important as the allocation of expenses is the amount of expenses. An addendum to the agreement should stipulate these expenses and indicate that the artist will only be liable for the expenses indicated on the addendum.

The artist needs to know what the total costs will be for each of the exhibition expenses. You don't want to pay half of the harpist's $500 fee for the opening party.

I am reminded of an artist's experience in her new gallery in Nantucket. It was her first solo show and the sales were fairly strong. She was shocked when she received her check, which was half of what she was expecting. It was the gallery's policy that the artist bears the brunt of show expenses, despite the fact she was never presented with an exhibition agreement.

Negotiation and agreements

All of the agreements between the gallery and the artist are usually straightforward, and the artist does not have to secure the services of an attorney to interpret the provisions. Unfortunately, some artists are so excited to find a new gallery that they barely scan the agreements. Now artists may not be able to negotiate every item in the agreement, but, at least, they should know what the agreement states.

The first three months is a critical time for the artist in a new gallery. If sales are not generated within this period, there is a very good probability they will never be generated.

12. The first three months

For the new artist (and the gallery), the first three months are critical in determining the success of the artist in the gallery. That success depends on generating sales in first 90 days. When a gallery takes on a new artist, they are enthusiastic and optimistic about the artist's sales potential. The gallery will usually place the artist's work in a desirable position on the gallery walls and will actively attempt to introduce the artist to their collectors. That enthusiasm and optimism will wane very quickly if sales do not quickly materialize.

A memorable case was a very popular and well-known west-coast artist who was recruited by our gallery. We all admired his work, and we were certain that he would sell well. We placed his work in the most prominent location in the gallery, and sent cards and emails announcing his addition to the gallery. For some reason, our collectors never responded enthusiastically to his work. In the first three months, we sold one painting, and that was to one major collector, who bought the piece more out of pity than for genuine enthusiasm for the work. The artist was not pleased because he sent some of his best pieces, and had been led to believe that sales would be significant. The relationship was quickly terminated to both the gallery's and the artist's relief.

The moral of this case is that regardless of the optimism that may surround the addition of a new artist, you never know how a new artist will perform in a gallery. And here's the rule that is rarely violated: if an artist does not sell in the first three months, the work will probably never sell.

Because these first three months are so critical, you must do everything you can do to assist sales. This includes supplying the new gallery with your best work, even if it means pulling pieces from other galleries. If you do not sell work, you want to know the reason. Was it because the gallery was a wrong fit or because you provided less than your best work? By supplying your best work, you have answered one of the questions.

If you cannot supply the gallery with your best work, then you are better off waiting until you can, for a gallery failure can have a very dispiriting effect on the artist.

If you cannot supply a new gallery with your best work, then you are better off waiting until you can, because failing at a gallery can have a very dispiriting effect on the artist. Plus, the art community is tight knit, and news of failures spreads just as easily as news of success.

In my own gallery, I have suggested to artists that rather than signing an agreement for an extended period, we look at the first three months as a trial. Then, if our collectors did not respond to the work, then we could end the experiment without any hard feelings. The art business is difficult enough without adding avoidable psychological trauma.

Besides sending strong work to the gallery, the artist can assist the gallery in other ways. For instance, the artist can volunteer to do a demo at the gallery. Also, the artist should note the new association on his or her website and social media pages. If the artist has collectors who reside near the new gallery, they should be emailed news regarding the new relationship, and perhaps sent images of the available work in the gallery.

I cannot understate the difficulty for the emerging artist to recruit new galleries. So when an artist has an opportunity to show in a new gallery, it is crucial to do everything that can be done to ensure the relationship will be successful. It makes no sense to seek galleries if you do not have quality work to provide the gallery. Less than your best work rarely succeeds even for the best artists.

*The gallery-artist
relationship is complex. It
is a business relationship
that usually evolves into
a personal relationship.
For the relationship to go
smoothly, both the business
and the personal aspects
must work.*

13. When things go wrong

The gallery-artist relationship is complex. It is a business relationship that usually evolves into a personal relationship. For the relationship to go smoothly and successfully, both the business and personal aspects must work.

As a rule of thumb, if the artist is selling one painting a month in most galleries, the gallery and the artist are normally satisfied. At certain destination galleries that attract hefty daily traffic that number may be higher. This doesn't mean that if an artist doesn't sell a piece every month that he or she will be asked to leave, but over the course of the year the artist should sell at least a dozen paintings.

If the artist is not selling a painting a month, the business side of the relationship is not working, and in most cases, it is best for both the artist and the gallery to terminate the relationship. Termination can be unpleasant so it is often postponed or avoided. In these cases of denial, the gallery stops showing the artist's pieces and/or the artist stops sending pieces.

Besides the awkwardness involved in terminating the relationship, there are other factors that explain this indecision. If the gallery is a prestigious one, the artist may be reluctant to pull out because of the prestige the gallery offers. And of course, if it is the artist's only gallery, it would be difficult for the artist to relinquish his or her only gallery outlet.

Similarly, if the artist is prestigious, then the gallery would like to retain the relationship for the prestige that the artist offers. Despite the obvious disappointment of such bad business relationships, I have seen such relationships last for years.

Business relationships can also deteriorate over time. It is not unusual for the artist's best-selling gallery to become the worst. This usually involves a change in personnel or direction within the gallery. I have often suggested to artist that if an artist does not have someone in the gallery who champions his or her work, then it is difficult to succeed in that gallery. When the artist's champion leaves the gallery, sales inevitably shrink.

Also, when management or ownership changes, it usually results in some change of direction for the gallery. These changes will favor a few and penalize a few, but the gallery's distribution of artists' sales will change. Even in situations where the new owners or managers intend to maintain the status quo, the composition of art sales can change. Gallery personalities not only have an effect on the artists, but also on the gallery's collectors as well. The artist's key collectors may not like the new owners, which will have an adverse effect on the artist's sales.

> *When management or ownership changes, it usually results in some change of direction for the gallery. These changes will favor a few and penalize a few, but the gallery's distribution of artists' sales will change.*

We represented an artist whose prime gallery was one in Taos. He was the gallery's top selling artist, and represented almost twenty percent of the sales volume for the gallery. When the gallery sold, he represented one of the key assets.

The new owners certainly intended to retain the artist, but dropped several artists whom the artist liked. This evoked some displeasure on his part and his personal relationship with the director deteriorated. Within a year he left the gallery despite continued sales. And when he left, several other prominent artists departed as well. The gallery closed the following year.

Even when sales are strong, the business relationship can suffer. Galleries can be notoriously bad in paying their artists. And nothing is more troubling for artists than having to chase the gallery to get paid for sales. Bad galleries may pay their major selling artists fairly promptly, but there are occasions when even the top artists discover the gallery has failed to pay them. Not only is this bad business practice, but it is a sure sign of financial difficulties. And if it is not a matter of finances, then it is a matter of scruples, and in either case, a reason to leave the gallery.

A related issue is the practice of excessive discounting without the artist's approval. Most gallery agreements call for limits on discounts without the artist's approval, but it is a common practice. Collectors expect discounts and some collectors demand heavy discounts. Many artists may be willing to allow a twenty percent discount, but they expect the gallery to at least notify them when the gallery discounts a sale. Many galleries routinely discount without notifying the artist, and expect the artist to accept the decision.

An artist friend had her Santa Fe gallery discount a piece 50%. When she expressed her anger, they gave her an ultimatum, which she refused. A week later they shipped back her paintings and a check for 25% of her sold piece.

In a perfect world, galleries would not have to discount

at all, but in the heat of negotiations, the gallery may have to discount to close the sale. Collectors can be fickle creatures, who can quickly cool to a potential purchase. We often discounted more than the 10% provided in our agreement, but it was our policy to take the discount from our commission. Most artists found this acceptable, but a few of our older established artists felt that any discount was an insult to them as artists. We certainly did not want to insult our artists so we would often lose sales. Some collectors believe it's an insult not to be offered a discount. Inflexible artists and collectors can make the gallery business very difficult.

The interpersonal relationship between the gallery and the artist are almost as important as the business relationship. If the artist and the gallery director do not share mutual respect, the relationship is always challenging. Like all interpersonal relationships, both parties make demands on the other. The gallery demands the artist to provide a certain kind of painting whereas the artist expects the gallery to generate sales. If there is no respect between the two parties, these demands can become very difficult.

> *The interpersonal relationship between the gallery and the artist is almost as important as the business relationship. If the artist and the gallery director do not share mutual respect, the relationship is always challenging.*

Now, it is also helpful if the artist and director are friendly or at least not unfriendly. As a gallery director, I once became crosswise with one of our artists. He had a national reputation and had a prior relationship with the owner of the gallery. It was not long before we despised each other to the point that he would disguise his voice when he called the gallery to talk to the owner. I had little enthusiasm to sell his work, and the rest of the gallery personnel including the owner ultimately followed suit. It was not much later that he pulled out of the gallery — much to my relief. The lesson here is that even in cases where the business relationship is positive, a negative interpersonal relationship inevitably results in the dissolution of the business relationship.

However, if the gallery director–artist relationship evolves into a friendship, this can present difficulties as well. Because of this mutual friendship, each will be reluctant to terminate a business relationship when sales fail to be generated. As I have noted earlier, when sales slow down, the artist will stop sending work and the gallery will stop hanging the artist's work. This situation can deteriorate, threatening even the friendship. It is better for both parties to shake hands and move on.

Whether it is a business or an interpersonal difficulty, when an artist decides to leave a gallery, it should be done immediately.

Whether it is because of a business or an interpersonal difficulty, when an artist decides to withdraw from a gallery, it should be done immediately. This is why it is important to have a short notification requirement in the gallery-artist agreement. Once it has become apparent to the gallery that the artist intends to leave, there is little incentive to show and sell the artist's work. The gallery may also be tempted to significantly discount the work and to even draw out payments for work sold. Of course not all galleries will lower themselves to such petty behavior, but some can be vindictive.

Regardless of the circumstances under which the artist leaves a gallery, the artist should resist the temptation to burn bridges. The art community is fairly tight-knit, and it is very easy for an artist to gain a reputation as being difficult even in situations when that reputation is not justified. When I interviewed artists who spent a great deal of effort to deprecate their former galleries, it raised red flags, and gave me concern about how difficult the artist would be. Gallery relationships are like all relationships and when they go bad, you need to move on and resist the temptation of becoming a victim of acrimony.

14. Alternatives to galleries

For the artists who do not want to sell their own work, there are alternatives to commercial galleries. None of these alternatives are sure-fire solutions, but all of them have been successful for some artists.

Artists' co-ops

For the emerging artist, there may be no better experience than to join an artist co-operative gallery. Since most co-ops require the artist to participate in manning the gallery, it provides the artist with some understanding into gallery operations and the behavior of collectors. Many artists do not appreciate the challenges that galleries face. The co-op experience provides insight into these difficulties.

In addition to the time commitment, the artist also has a financial commitment to the co-op. Monthly fees can range from a low of $25 to several hundred dollars. This can certainly be a difficult expense for emerging artists, but I think it can be well worth the investment. Not only does the co-op offer a place to show and hopefully sell work, but also it is an opportunity to be around other creative individuals. One of the real downsides of being an artist is the loneliness that is involved. It can be encouraging to know that you are not the only one facing the challenges of being an aspiring artist.

Most co-ops focus on the endeavor of creating art, and much less on the process of selling art. In some co-ops, the artist who succeeds in selling art may be viewed as "selling out," although deep-down every artist wants to sell. Nevertheless, this environment with an emphasis on creating instead of selling allows the artist to create art without worrying about its collector appeal. Of course, at some time in every artist's career, collector appeal becomes important.

There are professional art co-ops where selling art is prioritized. More traditional and experienced artists are usually found in these co-ops. Because of this, they are seeking others of their kind and especially artists who may have something of a collector base. They also have much less turnover in their artists, and thus, more difficult to join.

Joining a co-op can be like joining a church. You have to be concerned not only about the doctrine, but also the personality of its members.

Joining a co-op can be like joining a church. You have to be concerned not only by its doctrine, but also by the personality of its members. The best way to get a feel for the co-op is to visit their shows and even submit work for their open and juried shows. In addition to surveying the kind of art and the personalities in the co-op, one should also note the character of their collectors and if they actually buy art.

Participating in a co-op can be a rewarding experience especially for the emerging artist. However, don't expect to sell a lot of art and the price for the work will be substantially lower than you would see in a commercial gallery.

Rental galleries

A second opportunity for artists is to rent space in a gallery that offers space to artists. These may be pure art galleries or they can be mixed galleries offering other items such as jewelry and ceramics. Design and decoration centers also offer space to artists, and some are directed exclusively to professional designers and decorators. The monthly costs depends on the size of the space and the minimum investment is about $100.

Besides the monthly rental fee, these galleries also take a commission, which is usually about 20%. These staffs do not actively sell, so the artist has to rely on the inherent appeal of their work. There is also a potential issue of payment. Like art galleries, not all of these centers pay promptly.

Sales are dependent on the amount of traffic the venue attracts and the quality of its customers. Before renting space, you should visit the location on both the weekend and on weekdays. Besides surveying the traffic, the artist should evaluate the quality of visitor. Are these visitors potential buyers for your work?

It is important to also check out other art being shown in the venue. If the work is comparable to yours, you might contact the artists to see what their experience has been. Most artists will give you an honest review of their experience, but some may be reluctant to encourage another artist whose work competes with theirs. Perhaps, the best indicator of success is the length of time they have shown at the venue. If they have been with the venue a fairly long time, it is a good indication that the artist is at least making enough sales to pay the rent.

The results for rental galleries are mixed. There are some very successful art malls where sales have been very strong. However, in the majority of cases, if an artist covers his or her rental expense, he or she is doing much better than a majority of the other artists.

Art consultants and designers

I know an artist who makes a healthy five-figure income on sales to one art consultant. The artist is an abstract expressionist who paints large colorful canvases. She loves to experiment with composition and color, and never discards a painting even if she is not completely pleased with the outcome. A few years ago, she developed a relationship with one of Denver's most successful art consultants, who specialized in corporate accounts, both large and small. If one of the consultant's clients is seeking abstract work, the consultant knows the artist has a large inventory of potential work, and, more often than not, has a piece that will serve the client's needs. Although the artist only receives about a third for which the painting would sell in the gallery, she does not have to frame the work and avoids all of the logistic and interpersonal challenges that come with gallery representation. And because she is so prolific (she paints one or two large pieces a week), her volume of sales compensates for her lower prices.

> *Art consultants also offer another advantage in that they are more receptive to new artists than galleries. They are usually open to adding new artists and art to their portfolios.*

Art consultants offer another advantage in that they are much more receptive to new artists than galleries. The more diversity of art that consultants can offer their clients, the more success they will enjoy. Thus, they are usually always open to adding new artists and art to their portfolios. Perhaps even more important is that consultants favor artists who are not in galleries so their clients cannot compare the consultant's price with that of the galleries.

Even in a large city, the number of art consultants is usually fairly small, so the task of reaching them is not insurmountable. In most cases, it is sufficient to put together a package to include a portfolio sheet with representative samples of your work, a one-page bio, an information sheet, and a letter introducing yourself. The letter should invite the consultant to visit your studio to see the art in person. Also, the letter should indicate that a CD with additional images is available. After the material has been sent, you might follow up with a phone call to confirm that the material has been received, and again to extend the studio invitation.

Pricing to art consultants is a matter of negotiation. Like any negotiation the buyer (the consultant) is seeking the lowest price for the work and does not really care how much the artist sells the work to his or her collectors. The art consultant's profit depends on the margin between what they purchase art and what they sell it for. Some consultants add a fixed percentage to the purchase price, and some consultants price the art arbitrarily.

> *Pricing to art consultants is a matter of negotiation. Like any negotiation, the buyer is seeking the lowest price for the work and does not really care what the artist sells their work for to other buyers.*

The artist is rarely privy to what the consultant charges its clients. The fair price for the artist is what has been negotiated. Sometimes the consultant may sell the work for double or even more for what they paid the artist, but that's the consultant's business and the artist should accept it. Of course, renegotiation is possible, but the artist should resist this until the consultant has come to value the relationship.

Art consultants have clients who are seeking all genres of art so regardless of an artist's style and subject matter, consultants can be an attractive source of income. Normally, for this avenue to work, the artist has to be fairly prolific and be willing to sell work for less than they would receive in a gallery. Artists who paint small and slow are not good candidates.

Interior designers and decorators

It would seem that interior designers and decorators would also be a fertile ground for art sales. This is a false impression. In all of my years in the gallery business, we had targeted this group on many occasions, but not with great success. It is not that we did not make sales to this group, but they were spotty, and generally not worth the focus. That being said, we once sold a $50,000 painting through a designer. Just because this was not a fruitful market for us as a gallery, it does not necessarily mean that an artist may not have better luck.

I know several artists who significantly supplement their incomes with mural projects with many of these projects originating with designers. Murals can be very profitable projects, depending on the size and complexity of the mural. Although I find murals to be a valid art form, I am always surprised that many artists do not — including some muralists themselves.

Artists should approach designers and decorators as they would art consultants. It would not involve a great expense in time or money, but I am dubious of the potential of this market.

Artist brokers, agents, and consultants

I define an artist broker as an individual who sells art for in-dividual artists. This is opposed to art broker who purchases art for a client buyer. An artist broker can be a large company that represents artists to national design and decorator companies or it can be just one individual who sells the artist's work in a particular geographic area. Artist brokers usually take a smaller commission than do galleries, but the commission rate for some large companies can approach gallery commissions. Individual artist brokers may represent only a few artists, and sometimes only one

Art patrons can be regarded as unpaid artist brokers. An art patron purchases the artist's work primarily for the purpose of supporting the artist. An art patron can have a profound impact on an artist's career.

artist. Individual artist brokers rarely demands any exclusivity whereas the large companies may demand total exclusivity.

I have known artists who have had very successful relationships with artist brokers, and, of course, others who have not. I know one artist whose individual broker sold more art for her than the rest of her four galleries combined. I also have known artists who have done well financially with national brokers, but when an artist works with these brokers it is almost impossible to maintain any gallery relationships.

Besides the limitations imposed for potential galleries, the broker artists may begin to think of themselves as art factories where production and not quality becomes the major emphasis. Another problem, especially with national brokers is that you are totally dependent on their sales efforts. One last caveat: artists who paint exclusively for brokers can never be regarded as significant artists.

Note on art patrons

Art patrons can be regarded as unpaid artist brokers. An art patron purchases an artist's work primarily for the purpose of supporting the artist. Not only does the art patron purchase art, but they also promotes the artist's work to friends and family. Depending on the affluence of the patron's circle of friends, an art patron can have a profound impact on an artist's career. Much of Jackson Pollock's success can be attributed to the efforts of Peggy Guggenheim, who initially provided him with a monthly stipend. Of course, there are few artists to have such patrons.

Not all art patrons have to be as powerful and wealthy as Peggy Guggenheim. I have a friend who owns a small business and is only moderately affluent. Nevertheless, he has developed a patron relationship with a surrealist whose work he admires. He had agreed to purchase one painting a month for five years. The guaranteed sale has allowed the artist to paint full time, and if he becomes another Jackson Pollock, then my friend will have made a very good investment.

Artist consultants and agents

There is a belief among many artists that there is someone who can make them a star. And there are people who present themselves as star-makers. Some may even promise to find gallery representation for the artist. No gallery cares to work with artist reps, for galleries believe this is their role.

The artist-consultant relationship rarely works because the consultant makes promises that cannot be fulfilled. In most cases, the consultant becomes little more than a life coach. What most artists need are sales — not coaching.

15. Final thoughts

When I conduct my workshop, *Artist in Search of a Gallery*, I begin the workshop by telling the artists how difficult it is to get into galleries. I don't do this to discourage them, but to let them know the challenges they'll face. Most artists visit galleries on a regular basis and see that they are full of artists whose work may appear inferior to theirs. This leads to the false impression, "How difficult can this be? Although there are thousands of artists who show every day in American galleries, there are tens of thousands of artists who cannot find a gallery to represent them. Although we like to avoid the notion of competition among artists, in the case of the art business it is very real. In today's art scene, this has become a challenge even for established artists, and for the emerging artist the challenges are even greater.

Again, this observation is not to discourage artists, but to prepare them for what may be an arduous and difficult undertaking. I think for most artists gallery recruitment is the most disagreeable aspect of the art business. No one likes rejection, and when you pursue galleries, you will receive a lot of it. Even for the strongest of heart, continual rejection can affect your self-confidence as an artist. But the greatest of artists have faced similar rejection from before the Renaissance. The art business was not easy then, and it is certainly not easy now.

I have a very good friend who is an exceptionally talented artist and produces paintings that resonate with collectors.

Despite enjoying success in most every gallery he has ever shown in, he is now finding it difficult to replace the galleries that have closed on him. Several galleries where his work is obviously superior to most of the artists showing in these galleries have rejected him. Even he is beginning to question his ability as an artist.

As a gallery owner and director, I thought I was a pretty good judge of what constituted good art, and what had real "salability." I suspect all gallery directors and owners feel the same way. But to be perfectly honest, I have encountered gallery directors whose taste in art and artists seemed clueless. This is often confirmed when these people serve as jurors for shows. In fact, being rejected by these people may actually serve as a badge of honor.

I think this book provides the artist with the most effective knowledge for pursuing a gallery. That does not mean that every reader will find success after reading the book, but, hopefully, he or she will feel that they did it "the right way." As I've noted in the first chapter, an artist can find success without gallery representation. For many artists this is the right path. Although selling you own art is not a simple matter either, it can often be less frustrating than dealing with galleries.

Finally, there are people who should not worry about selling art at all. It is not that they are not fine artists, but that the process of selling deprives them of the joy of creating art. In some ways I feel these are the true artists, and the ones I respect greatly.

Whatever choices and directions the artist chooses, I wish he or she well, because the life of the artist is not for the fainthearted.

Appendices

The Gallery-Artist
Representation Agreement

The gallery-artist agreement outlines the rules by which the gallery and the artist are to conduct their business. It is a legally enforceable agreement which is seldom enforced. Galleries routinely ignore the provisions, and artists overlook this disregard. Still, the agreement describes the way the parties should conduct business.

The following agreement is a sample of an such agreement with annotations for many of the provisions. This agreement is slanted favorably toward the artist, whereas other agreements might be more favorable to the gallery.

Gallery-Artist Representation Agreement

Agreement

This agreement is between the ARTIST and the GALLERY indicated below.

ARTIST   GALLERY

_____   _____
Name   *Name*

_____   _____
Street   *Street*

_____   _____
City, State, Zip   *City, State, Zip*

1. Representation

The ARTIST hereby appoints the GALLERY as agent for the works of art ("Artworks") consigned to the gallery, for the purposes of exhibition and sale. The GALLERY shall not permit the artworks to be used for any other purposes without the written consent of the ARTIST. This agreement applies only to Artworks consigned to the GALLERY, and does not make the GALLERY a general agent for any other works.

2. Exclusivity

The ARTIST appoints the GALLERY as its exclusive representative within the following area: _____.

The area may be defined by state e.g. "Texas" or by city, "Austin, Texas and 100 miles circumference of Austin." The wider the defined area the more control the artist is relinquishing. For instance, the Austin designation would preclude a gallery in San Antonio.

If the gallery is located in the artist's region, the artist is giving up the opportunity to participate in some local shows. Thus, the provision might include a waiver for certain shows in which the artist would like to participate.

Nor does the provision directly address the issue of the artist selling artwork out of his or her studio. If the artist has developed a significant volume of studio sales, this should be addressed in this provision.

3. Term of Agreement

The term of this agreement will be for _____ months from the time of this signed document. This agreement will terminate with the death of the ARTIST or sale of the GALLERY.

This allows the artist to pull out of a gallery that sells to new owners who may move the gallery into a new direction.

4. Termination of Agreement

Either party may terminate this agreement with _____ days of written notice.

The notice is usually between 30 and 90 days. A short termination period favors the artist. No artist wants to remain in a gallery that is not longer interested in selling the artist's work.

5. Warranty

The ARTIST hereby warrants that he/she created and possesses unencumbered title to the artworks, and that their descriptions are true and accurate.

6. Shipping

Packing and shipping charges, insurance and other handling expenses, and risk of loss or damage incurred in the delivery of Artworks from the ARTIST to the GALLERY are the responsibility of the ARTIST. Packing and shipping charges, insurance and other handling expenses, and risk of loss or damage incurred in the delivery of Artworks from the GALLERY to the ARTIST are the responsibility of the GALLERY.

7. Fiduciary Responsibility

Title to each of the Artworks remains with the ARTIST until the ARTIST has been paid the full amount owing him or her for the Artworks; title then passes directly to the purchaser. All proceeds from the sale of Artworks shall be held in trust for the ARTIST. The GALLERY shall pay all amounts due the ARTIST before any proceeds of sales can be made available to creditors of the GALLERY.

This states the artist has priority over other creditors of the gallery. This may be contested by the other creditors and is not always supported in court.

8. Responsibility for Loss or Damage

The GALLERY shall be responsible for the safekeeping of all consigned Artworks while in its custody. The GALLERY shall be strictly liable to the ARTIST for their loss or damage except for damage resulting from flaws inherent in the Artworks. The GALLERY shall not lend out, remove from the premises, or sell on approval any of the Artworks without first obtaining written permission from the ARTIST.

This is another provision that is not always abided by the gallery. Galleries always allow their collectors to take home paintings "on approval," and rarely do they contact their artists for approval. The artist is protected by payment guarantees in the payment provision.

Frame damage is another significant issue for artists. Normal gallery activity will result in some degradation in the frames. The question is how damaged are the frames and what is the cost to have them repaired. Artists who complain about frame damage may receive some compensation from the gallery, but the complaining can jeopardize their standing in the gallery.

Damage to the actual paintings rarely occurs and should be covered by the gallery's insurance, although most galleries are reluctant to make claims for fear of raising their rates. Some agreements will state that the artist will receive an amount equal to what they would have received in the painting had sold.

9. Insurance Coverage

The GALLERY shall provide adequate insurance coverage for all Artworks. The GALLERY will provide information regarding this coverage upon request of the ARTIST.

Artists always assume the galleries carry adequate insurance and will rarely inquire about the insurance. Most galleries start out with insurance, but for struggling galleries, it is often one of the first expenses to be reduced or cut.

10. Notice of Consignment

The GALLERY shall give notice by means of a clear and conspicuous sign in full public view that consigned Artworks are being sold subject to a contract of consignment.

I have never seen a notice of consignment in any gallery that I have ever visited nor has any artist every questioned why the gallery did not have such a notice.

11. Reproduction

The ARTIST reserves all right to the reproduction of the Artworks except as noted in writing. The GALLERY will not permit any of the Artworks to be copied, photographed or reproduced without the written permission of the ARTIST. In those instances where permission has been granted, the ARTIST shall be acknowledged as the creator and the copyright owner of the Artworks. The GALLERY shall include on each bill of sale of any Artworks the following legend: "All rights to reproduction of the work(s) of art identified herein are retained by the ARTIST (Artist's name)."

The legend that is noted above is rarely seen on bill of sales to buyers, but some collectors are under the belief that they own rights to the image.

12. Framing

If the GALLERY frames the Artwork, the GALLERY and the ARTIST agree that the cost of framing will be included in the price and the gallery will be compensated for these costs. Should the Artworks be returned to the ARTIST, the GALLERY and the ARTIST will be equally responsible for the wholesale cost of the framing.

13. Pricing

The GALLERY will sell Artworks at the retail price specified on the consignment sheets. The GALLERY will only discount the price with the ARTIST'S permission.

14. Gallery Commission

The gallery commission will be _____% of the sales price of the Artworks.

15. Payment

For all sales during the month, the GALLERY will pay the ARTIST by the 15th day of the following month. The GALLERY assumes full risk for the failure to pay on the part of the purchaser for any Artwork.

16. Accounting

The ARTIST shall have the right to inventory his or her Artworks in the GALLERY, and to inspect any books and records pertaining to sales of Artworks.

17. Modification

Amendments to the agreement must be signed by both the ARTIST and the GALLERY and attached to this agreement. Both parties must initial any deletions made on this form and additional provisions added to it.

18. Miscellaneous

This agreement represents the entire agreement between the ARTIST and the GALLERY. If any part of this agreement is held to be illegal or unenforceable, such holding will not effect the validity of the balance of the agreement. This agreement shall not be assigned without prior written consent of the ARTIST.

19. Choice of Laws

This agreement shall be covered by the laws of the state of

_____.

Date: _____

_____   _____
Artist   Gallery

The Gallery-Artist Exhibition Agreement

The gallery-artist exhibition agreement outlines the responsibilities of both the gallery and the artist regarding the presentation of an exhibition. Many of the provisions in an exhibition agreement are the same as in a representation agreement. Most exhibition agreements are not as comprehensive as the example given here, but it will include many of the same provisions that are in this agreement.

When a gallery represents an artist, they rarely provide an exhibition agreement, but for the same reasons that warrant a representational agreement apply to an exhibition agreement.

Gallery-Artist Exhibition Agreement

Agreement

This agreement is between the ARTIST and the GALLERY indicated below.

ARTIST   GALLERY

_____   _____
Name   *Name*

_____   _____
Street   *Street*

_____   _____
City, State, Zip   *City, State, Zip*

1. Purpose

The ARTIST agrees to provide "Artworks" for the exhibition "Name of the exhibition" produced by the GALLERY. The ARTIST understands the exhibition will be a solo/group exhibition.

This agreement is between the artist and the gallery producing the show. In many cases the exhibition will be produced by an individual or organization other than the gallery, but the issues and provisions are the same.

2. Dates

The exhibition will be presented [Opening Date] through [Closing date]

3. Artworks

The ARTIST agrees to supply the GALLERY a minimum of _____ pieces, and a maximum of _____ pieces. The GALLERY reserves the right to reject any work that does not meet the standards of the exhibition. The ARTIST agrees to allow the gallery to retain all consigned Artworks for the duration of the show. All Artworks must be available for sale.

4. Warranty

The ARTIST hereby warrants that he/she created and possesses unencumbered title to the Artworks, and that their descriptions are true and accurate.

5. Shipping

Packing and shipping charges, insurance and other handling expenses, and risk of loss or damage incurred in the delivery of Artworks from the ARTIST to the GALLERY are the responsibility of the ARTIST. Packing and shipping charges, insurance and other handling expenses, and risk of loss or damage incurred in the delivery of Artworks from the GALLERY to the ARTIST are the responsibility of the ARTIST. The ARTIST is responsible for the arrangement for returning shipping.

Artworks from the ARTIST must arrive at the GALLERY at least 14 days before the opening date and no more than 28 days. The ARTIST has 7 days after the close of the exhibition to pickup work or have them picked up by their designated shipper.

The artist is usually responsible for shipping costs to and from the location. If the artist is represented by the gallery, the gallery may elect to keep some of the show pieces after the show.

6. Framing

The ARTIST will provide the GALLERY with Artworks which are properly framed and wired for hanging.

This is usually not an issue for artists already represented by the gallery, but it can be a real issue when the artist has never exhibited with the gallery.

7. Reproduction

The ARTIST reserves all rights to the reproduction of the Artworks except as noted in writing. The GALLERY will not permit any of the Artworks to be copied, photographed or reproduced without the written permission of the ARTIST. In those instances where permission has been granted, the ARTIST shall be acknowledged as the creator and the copyright owner of the Artworks. The GALLERY shall include on each bill of sale of any Artworks the following legend: "All rights to reproduction of the works of art identified herein are retained by the ARTIST (Artist's name).

8. Insurance Coverage

The GALLERY shall provide adequate insurance coverage for all Artworks. The GALLERY will provide information regarding this coverage upon request of the ARTIST.

9. Responsibility for Loss or Damage

The GALLERY shall be responsible for the safekeeping of all consigned Artworks while in its custody. The GALLERY shall be strictly liable to the ARTIST for their loss or damage except for damage resulting from flaws inherent in the Artworks. The GALLERY shall not lend out, remove from the premises, or sell on approval of any of the Artworks without first obtaining written permission from the ARTIST.

10. Pricing

The GALLERY will sell Artworks at the retail price specified on the consignment sheets. The GALLERY will only discount the price with the ARTIST'S permission.

11. Gallery Commission

The gallery commission will be _____% of the sales price of the Artworks.

The commission for shows is usually the same for a represented artist, but for other artists, the commission can widely range. If the artist is paying a rental fee as part of the exhibition, the commission is usually much lower, and occasionally no commission at all is paid.

12. Payment

For all sales during the exhibition, the GALLERY will pay the ARTIST by the 15th day after the closing of the show. The GALLERY assumes full risk for the failure to pay on the part of the purchaser for any Artwork.

If the show is scheduled to run for several months, this may represent a financial hardship for the artist to have to wait for payment after the show closes. The gallery or producer usually collects payment at the time of purchase, but galleries may allow some collectors to postpone payment until work is picked up.

13. Expenses

The expenses for the exhibition will be proportioned accordingly:

a. Advertising: GALLERY: 50%; ARTIST: 50%

b. Invitation preparation, printing and mailing:

GALLERY: 50%; ARTIST: 50%

c. Opening Reception: GALLERY 100%; ARTIST: 0%

d. Miscellaneous expenses: GALLERY: 100%; ARTIST: 0%

The GALLERY will provide an itemized sheet of projected expenses to the ARTIST. The itemized sheet must be signed by both the ARTIST and the GALLERY. Furthermore, any expenses beyond those included on the itemized sheet or exceeding the projected expenses will be assumed by the GALLERY unless such expenses are authorized in writing by the ARTIST.

For artists with a solo show this is the most important provision in the agreement. Unexpected expenses can certainly limit the financial success of a show. Many artists have learned this lesson the hard way. It also forces the gallery to examine their potential expenses as well, The percentages presented above are typical for most exhibitions, but some galleries may expect all of the opening reception expenses to be responsibility of the artist, and it is normally always the case when the artist rents the gallery space.

14. Accounting and inspection

The ARTIST shall have the right to inspect any books and records pertaining to sales of Artworks.

In the case of the representational agreement, this can be a very sticky issue. It is the same for the exhibition agreement. Many galleries and producers will routinely provide this information to the artist, but not all.

15. Modification

Amendments to this agreement must be signed by both the ARTIST and the GALLERY and attached to this agreement. Both parties must initial any changes to this agreement.

16. *Miscellaneous*

This agreement represents the entire agreement between the ARTIST and the GALLERY. If any part of this agreement is held to be illegal or unenforceable, such holding will not effect the validity of the balance of the agreement. This agreement shall not be assigned without prior written consent of the ARTIST.

17. *Choice of Laws*

This agreement shall be covered by the laws of the state of

_____.

Date: _____

_____   _____
Artist   Gallery

Consignment Sheet

The consignment sheet should not be confused with a consignment agreement, which is basically a gallery-artist representation agreement.

The consignment sheet is the artist's and the gallery's record of paintings received by the gallery. In most cases, the gallery has its own consignment sheet which it provides the artist when he or she drops off work at the gallery. Unfortunately, galleries are not always diligent in providing the artist with a consignment sheet.

It is in the best interest of artists to have their own consignment sheets to insure proper record-keeping for all of their inventory in the gallery.

Art Consignment Sheet

Receipt

The gallery or organization indicated below acknowledges the receipt of the following art.

Title	Medium	Size	Retail Price

Commission and responsibilities are not indicated on the consignment sheet because these should be covered in either the gallery-artist representation agreement or the exhibition agreement. If such agreements are not in place then the commission rate may also be included on this art consignment sheet. Art titles can be redundant and therefore confusion can occur, so I recommend that artists should always assign a unique code for each of their paintings. That code should be indicated on the consignment sheet either in parenthesis after the title or in a separate column.

Date _____

Gallery Name   Artist Name

_____   _____

Gallery Signature   *Artist Signature*

_____   _____

Websites of interest

artistinsearch.innovativebooks.net

This is the official support site for *To the Artist in Search of a Gallery* with support for the following chapters.

Chapter 2: Are You Ready?

Links to popular publication websites for artists as well as some interesting art and artist blogs.

Chapter 3: Requisites for the artist

Links to sources for different products and services helpful to the artist.

Chapter 9: Does advertising work?

Links to art collector publications.

Appendices

PDFs:
1. Gallery-artist representation agreement,
2. Gallery-artist exhibition agreement.
3. Art consignment sheet.

artistswatch.com

ArtistsWatch.com is a free promotional site that exposes artists to hundreds of American art galleries.

Cover

The King's Jester
By William Merritt Chase

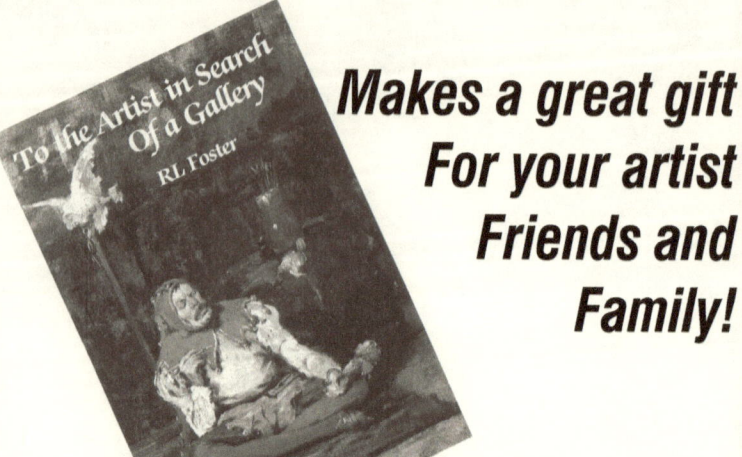